The Birds Eye book of

Britain's favourite recipes

The Birds Eye book of

Britain's favourite recipes

by Ambrose Heath

Book two

© Birds Eye Foods Limited 1964

Published by Wolfe Publishing Limited, 10 Welbeck
   Way, London W1, for Birds Eye Foods Limited,
   Walton-on-Thames, Surrey

Photography by Robert Gibb

Printed by Smeets Lithographers, Weert, The Netherlands

Phototypeset by Filmset Limited, Fleming Way,
   Crawley, Sussex

Bound by Bookprint Limited, Kingswood, Surrey

Designed by Elwyn Blacker, MSIA

The food photographed in these books was prepared in the
   creative kitchens of Birds Eye Foods Limited, Walton-on-
   Thames, by the Home Economics staff.

Contents

All quantities in this book, unless otherwise stated, are for four people

ACKNOWLEDGEMENTS

The publishers express their grateful thanks to the following for the provision of articles used in photography:

China: Heal and Son Ltd, Royal Worcester Porcelain Co Ltd, Rosenthal (London) Ltd, Josiah Wedgwood and Sons Ltd, Peter Knight (Esher) Ltd, Derek Holmes, Walton-on-Thames

Pottery: Josiah Wedgwood and Sons Ltd

Cutlery: British Silverware Ltd

Glass: Glass Manufacturers' Federation, J. Wuidart and Co Ltd

Linen: Heal and Son Ltd, Robinson and Cleaver Ltd

Introduction

In Volume One we have tried to give you a useful, no-nonsense, everyday cookery book. Some of it is perhaps already well established in your experience, but there are always new ways of getting the best and most attractive results from your cooking.

Frankly, we stretched a point to include some interesting dishes that are not perhaps yet fully naturalised, but at least they are well on the way to being among Britain's favourites.

For Volume Two we have also allowed some interesting foreigners to creep in, but we think you'll agree with us that they certainly deserve their place among the favourites, too.

Where Volume One dealt with the more interesting end of everyday cooking, with a lot of the preparation cut out, in Volume Two we have looked at food for the special occasion. But only you can say what is a special occasion. It may be a birthday party; perhaps the boss is coming to dinner; or perhaps you've just bought a new hat and want your husband extra well fed before you tell him!

Whatever the reason, if it is worth that little extra time and trouble, let Volume Two be your guide. With these recipes your family will certainly eat well, and we think you'll get away with that hat!

Author's introduction

The first volume of Britain's Favourite Recipes has been devoted in the main to the actual business of cooking. This second one contains a collection of additional recipes which, in the opinion of the compiler, are representative of the most acceptable today in our national cooking.

To these have been added a number of foreign dishes, from France, America, Italy, Russia, Hungary, Scandinavia, the Near East and India, which have already been adopted by our kitchens or are in process of acclimatisation.

Cookery is a fluid art and is continually increasing in scope and interest in the kitchens of every nationality according to whatever opportunities, or new methods or ingredients present themselves as time goes on. The main thing is to enjoy them, which I hope readers will do.

Soups

The British people, unlike Continental nations, have never been particularly soup-conscious. Soups have always been considered part of a meal and not, like their European counterparts, an opportunity for a substantial meal in themselves, with the result that we have actually produced only a very small number of different kinds.

In this short section a small number of such soups are described, and I should like to draw special attention to the simple fish soup and the more exotic lobster soup and the three attractive vegetable soups made from onion, green peppers and watercress respectively. The section on the different garnishes which will help to enliven the home-made or tinned consommé should also be found useful when entertaining.

BEETROOT SOUP

This pleasant soup, if finished with cream, is such a pretty pink that the colour itself is quite an appetiser.

3 beetroots : 1 head celery : $\frac{1}{2}$ pint milk : $\frac{1}{2}$ pint water : salt and pepper.

Bake the beetroots in a pan of water for three hours, then peel them and chop them up with the celery. Put the milk and water into a saucepan and cook the vegetable mixture in this until soft enough to rub through a sieve.

Do this and finish the soup with a spoonful or two of cream and a few little bits of butter.

Sprinkle with minced parsley.

CAULIFLOWER SOUP

The secret of this soup is the addition of the bayleaf, which gives it an unexpected flavour.

1 cauliflower : 1 small onion : 1 stick of celery : 2 oz. butter : 1 bay leaf : 1 oz. flour : 2 pints white stock : 1 pint milk.

Cook the cauliflower (no leaves) in boiling salted water for twenty minutes and then cut it in half. Keep one half warm and rub the other through a rather coarse sieve. Chop a small onion and the stick of celery (or when the latter is not available, season with celery salt) and fry them lightly, without colouring them, in the butter with a bay leaf. Take out the bay leaf and stir in an ounce of flour. Cook for a minute or two and then moisten with two pints of white stock, stirring well. Meanwhile boil up a pint of milk and mix the sieved cauliflower with it. Pour into the stock and strain through a coarse sieve just to get rid of the pieces of celery and onion. Garnish with the other half of the cauliflower broken into small pieces, sprinkle at the very last with chopped parsley or chervil, and hand fried bread croûtons with it.

CHESTNUT SOUP

To those who like chestnuts a soup made with them sometimes comes as a pleasant new experience.

4 doz. chestnuts : 2 small onions : 1 carrot : 2 leeks : $\frac{1}{4}$ head celery : 1 oz. butter : 3 or 4

cloves : 1 quart milk or milk and water : salt and pepper.

Fry the finely chopped vegetables in the butter until lightly browned, then add the milk or milk and water, the cloves to taste and a little salt and simmer gently for an hour.

Meanwhile shell and skin the chestnuts and stew them gently in half of the liquid for half an hour or until tender, take out a few whole ones to use as a garnish and chop up the rest and rub them with their liquid through a fine sieve. Add to this the rest of the liquid, strained, from the first cooking, and stew on together for another ten minutes or so. Serve garnished with the re-served nuts whole or broken in largish pieces and sprinkled with chopped parsley.

CONSOMMÉ ROYALE

This famous soup is a clear consommé, descri-bed on page 19 of Volume One, with a garnish of custard made with stock instead of milk. 1 egg-yolk : 2 tablespoonfuls good well-seasoned strained white stock.

Heat the stock to blood heat (98° F), pour it over the beaten egg-yolk, stirring all the time, season further if necessary and strain into a but-tered cup or other container. Cover this with buttered greaseproof paper or kitchen foil and either steam very gently or bake in a cool oven in a tin of water for twenty minutes to half an hour. When completely set, turn this royale out on a plate, let it get quite cold and then cut it into fancy shapes. Leave these in cold water until required, then take them out and warm them by pouring a little hot water over them. Lastly, drain off the water, put the pieces of royale into the soup tureen and pour the hot consommé over them.

Some like to use a little cream with the stock in making these little garnishes, but the total amount of liquid must not exceed an eighth of a pint.

COCKLE SOUP

A cheap shellfish soup of some attraction.

1 quart measure cockles : $\frac{3}{4}$ oz. butter : $\frac{3}{4}$ oz. flour : $\frac{1}{2}$ pint milk : 2 sticks celery : parsley.

Scrub the cockles well and boil them in salted water until they open. Drain off the liquid and keep it aside. Make a white roux with the butter and flour and moisten it smoothly with a pint of the cockle water and the milk. Add now the chopped celery, simmer for half an hour and then add the shelled cockles, some chopped parsley and salt and pepper to taste. Cook for a few minutes longer before serving.

CREAM OF BARLEY SOUP

A very delicious old-fashioned soup if you use well-flavoured chicken stock to make it.

2 oz. pearl barley : 1 oz. butter : 1 small onion : 1 small carrot : 1 stick celery : 1 quart chicken stock : 1 egg-yolk : salt, pepper and grated nut-meg : fried bread croûtons.

Wash the barley and blanch it by putting it into cold water and just bringing to the boil. Lightly fry the vegetables, cut small, in the butter and then add the drained barley and the stock.

Cook gently for a couple of hours, and then strain. Season with a touch of nutmeg, salt and pepper, and thicken with the egg-yolk without letting the soup boil. Sprinkle with chopped parsley and hand fried bread croûtons with it.

CUCUMBER SOUP

A lovely light soup for summertime and so easy to make.

1 medium cucumber: $\frac{1}{2}$ oz. butter: 2 large spring onions: salt, pepper, grated nutmeg and cayenne pepper: 2 egg-yolks: 2 tablespoonfuls cream; chervil if possible, otherwise parsley.

Peel the cucumber, cut it into thin slices and toss these in the butter for a few minutes to soften them. Take them out and keep them warm in another pan, while in the same butter fry the sliced onions very lightly. Now add these to the cucumber and pour over boiling water (it must be water and not stock or milk) to cover the vegetables by a good inch. Season with salt, pepper, a little grated nutmeg and a touch of cayenne pepper and simmer for about half an hour until the liquid has reduced by a third. Then thicken with the yolks beaten in the cream without letting the soup boil.

Serve sprinkled with chopped chervil, if you can get it, otherwise with parsley.

GREEN SWEET PEPPER SOUP

Green sweet peppers have risen during the last few years right to the top of the British gastronomical table, and recipes for them proliferate almost weekly in all the magazines. Here, however, is something rather different.

Fry two tablespoonfuls of chopped onion and three of chopped green pepper in two ounces of butter for five minutes without browning them. Mix in an ounce and a half of flour and then a pound of quartered tomatoes and a quart of brown stock and simmer for about half an hour.

Now rub the whole thing through a sieve and season highly with salt, pepper and cayenne pepper.

If you like, you can serve this delicious soup just as it is, but the wise will add at the last a very small dash of vinegar and a little grated horseradish (or a small teaspoonful of horseradish sauce) and some thin rings of cooked macaroni. It tastes just as exotic as it sounds.

HOLLANDAISE SOUP

Another delicious light soup for summertime, for which you will need one of those little metal scoops that cut vegetables into pieces the size and shape of green peas.

1 cucumber: 3 or 4 carrots: 1 oz. butter: $\frac{3}{4}$ oz. flour: $1\frac{1}{2}$ pints white stock, preferably chicken: 2 egg-yolks: $\frac{1}{4}$ pint cream: a few cooked or frozen green peas.

Scoop out enough little balls from the carrots 141

Hollandaise soup

and peeled cucumber to fill a half pint measure and boil them in salted water until tender. Melt the butter, mix with the flour and stir in by degrees the stock, which should be good and well-flavoured as the soup depends on this, the vegetables being only a garnish.

When the soup has cooked, skim it and thicken it with the egg-yolks mixed with the cream. Then add the drained carrot and cucumber balls and lastly a few tablespoonfuls of the peas and half a teaspoonful of chopped parsley.

The colours of the vegetables just veiled by the light golden liquid could not be nicer.

LOBSTER SOUP

One hen lobster : 1 quart fish stock : 1 onion : sprig of thyme, parsley and bay leaf : 2 oz. butter : 2 oz. flour : 1 teaspoonful anchovy essence : $\frac{1}{8}$ pint cream.

Take out the flesh from the cooked lobster and pound the shell. When making the fish stock, add this shell.

Fry the onion and herbs lightly in the butter, then sprinkle in the flour and cook on until it is a pale-fawn colour. Add the strained stock and cook gently for three-quarters of an hour.

Rub the coral of the lobster which you will recognise of course by its colour—coral, with

Lobster soup

half an ounce of butter through a fine sieve, add it to the soup and then add the anchovy essence and cream, with a touch of lemon juice. Serve some of the lobster flesh in the soup, which some like coloured with a very little carmine colouring.

ONION SOUP

The English cook's idea of this fragrant soup used to be a rather more liquid form of onion sauce, but of recent years the more discerning have adopted the simpler and more appetising French version. Quantities vary to taste.

Cut the onions in thin slices and fry these in a little butter until they are tender and golden coloured. Pour in enough boiling water so that, when it is reduced by cooking by a third, the right quantity of soup will remain. When the soup is seasoned, especially with freshly ground black pepper, the easiest and best way to serve it is just as it is with grated cheese handed.

SPINACH SOUP

Prepare some spinach by removing the midribs and washing the leaves well, melt an ounce of butter in a saucepan and in this cook the spinach slowly with half a dozen finely chopped spring onions until soft. Frozen spinach can of course be used. Now chop the spinach finely and add to it about three-quarters of a pint of hot water, and simmer gently for half an hour.

Now add half a pint of milk and go on boiling until the soup is suitably reduced. Bind before serving with egg-yolk beaten up in a little cream. In addition to the usual salt-and-pepper seasoning a little grated nutmeg is always welcome with this vegetable. 143

WATERCRESS SOUP

A fresh spring-like soup which is by no means sufficiently well-known.

1 lb. old potatoes : 1 small bunch watercress : 1 egg-yolk : 2 tablespoonfuls cream.

Three-quarters cook the thickly sliced potatoes in enough very slightly salted water to cover them, and then add the watercress well washed and chopped up, reserving a few whole leaves for the garnish. Cook on until the potatoes are done, then rub the whole thing through a sieve. Thin down if necessary with a little water and simmer a while longer, seasoning with a little pepper.

Finish with the egg-yolk beaten in the cream to thicken it.

It is one of the best light soups there are, but you must be certain to use only water, as no flavoured liquid like stock should be allowed to interfere with the fresh taste of the watercress.

GARNISHES FOR CONSOMMÉS

There are a number of garnishes that will make a plain consommé look more exciting, and the simplest of these are colourings of the royale which is described on page 140.

This savoury custard, as indeed it is, can be flavoured and coloured by adding various purées of cooked vegetables, taking care that the total amount of liquid including this addition does not amount to more than one-eighth of a pint for the eggs specified. Hence a purée of the red part of carrot will turn it pink, tinned tomato purée red, purée of spinach or watercress green, or the plain royale could be flavoured with mixed herbs, celery salt, etc. A mixture of several kinds of these little dice in one consommé is very pretty indeed.

As for other garnishes, there are numberless little pasta in the shape of tiny shells, stars, wheels, letters of the alphabet and so on, the most familiar to our great-grandmothers being the very thin almost hair-like vermicelli. These pasta have, of course, to be cooked in salted water separately first, as if they were cooked in the consommé itself, they would risk clouding it.

Other garnishes, where suitable, are strips of cooked celery : strips of the white part of cooked chicken ; thin strips of cooked ham and tomato flesh ; green peas ; cooked carrots and turnips cut pea-shaped with a special scoop ; cooked asparagus tips ; diamond shapes of cooked green beans and, more solidly, very thin strips of cooked savoury pancake cut after it has been rolled up.

All these garnishes are added to the soup itself, but here is a popular one which is always handed separately.

Diablotins.

Cut some little rounds of stale bread an inch in diameter and an eighth of an inch thick, butter them, spread them with grated cheese mixed with a little cayenne pepper, which is raised in a solid dome upon each. Then bake them in a hot oven until the cheese is browned.

Hors d'oeuvre

The hors d'oeuvre course is a comparatively recent innovation in British homes, but it is well acclimatised by now and there must be few readers who are not familiar with the usual little dishes of sardines, anchovies, potted shrimps, potato salad, liver pâté, salami and so on which decorate so many tables.

The short list that follows is intended to offer something a little out of the ordinary but, in these days of frozen and tinned foods and continental delicatessen shops, quite easy to prepare.

ANCHOVY AND HAM CANAPÉS

Get some thinnest possible slices of cooked ham and butter them carefully using a warmed knife. Drain some anchovy fillets in oil and roll up each of these in a strip of the ham, like a cigarette. Serve cold on fingers of buttered toast.

ANCHOVY PAUPIETTES

Flatten some drained anchovy fillets in oil slightly, beating them with the back of a wooden spoon, and spread each with a little of a purée of cooked white fish moistened with mayonnaise. Then roll up each fillet and serve them side by side in a long dish.

SWEDISH CANAPÉS

Make these with buttered brown bread (black bread if you can get it from your delicatessen shop) instead of the usual toast, and spread each with butter pounded with a little grated horseradish, and surmount this by a thin slice of smoked salmon, fresh or tinned in oil. Finish with a drop of lemon juice.

ANCHOVIES AND SWEET PEPPERS

Drain the anchovy fillets well and cut them into short thin strips. Do the same to some tinned sweet red peppers, mix them lightly together and finish with a few drops of olive oil.

BEETROOT

Cut the cooked beetroot into short thin strips and mix it with very thin rings of spring onions. Dress with a mixture of lemon juice and cream seasoned with French mustard, salt and pepper and made in the same way and in the same proportions as oil-and-vinegar dressing, the cream taking the place of the oil and the lemon of the vinegar.

This dressing is called mustard sauce with cream.

CAULIFLOWER

Cut the cauliflower into little flowerets and half-cook them in salted water. When quite cold let them lie for an hour or so in a mixture of two parts olive oil and one part vinegar, drain them well and serve them in a mustard sauce with cream.

CELERIAC

Peel and cut the celeriac, raw, into very thin, short strips indeed, and serve it dressed either with a mustard sauce with cream or with an oil-and-vinegar dressing touched with mustard.

CELERY AND APPLE

Chop up equal parts of celery and dessert apple and dress with mustard sauce with cream.

DANISH CUCUMBER

Peel the cucumber and cut it into thickish rounds. Scoop out almost all of the centres, leaving just a thin layer at the bottom of the piece, and fill the hollows with a mixture of smoked salmon and hard-boiled eggs cut in little dice. Cover with a little grated horseradish and serve very cold.

FRENCH OR RUNNER BEANS

Be careful not to overcook them, for they should still have a 'bite' in them. Drain them well and dress them with oil-and-vinegar while they are still hot, and when they get cold serve them with chopped parsley and spring onion green on top.

MUSSELS

Drain some tinned or bottled mussels and mix them with thin short strips of celery.

Dress with mustard sauce with cream made as for beetroot on page 145.

EGG MAYONNAISE

Hard-boil as many eggs as you want, and let them get cold. Then cut them in halves lengthways and arrange them in a shallow dish.

Pour a thickish creamy mayonnaise sauce over them, and serve very cold.

Variations may be made by criss-crossing the rounded part of the eggs (after the mayonnaise has been poured over) with very thin strips of anchovy fillets or of smoked salmon. In the case of the former each interstice may contain one caper, and in the latter a very tiny sprig of parsley or one or two threads of fresh dill or fennel, if you can get them.

CELERY AND BEETROOT

Cut some celery into thin strips and some cooked beetroot as well, draining the latter after cutting. Mix lightly together and bind with Tartare sauce (Volume One, page 26).

SMOKED COD'S ROE CANAPÉS

The canapés are made with brown bread, not toast, and they are spread generously with smoked cod's roe pounded with butter and a

touch of cayenne pepper. A squeeze of lemon is added at the end with a decoration of finely minced parsley.

COD'S ROE PÂTÉ

A Greek hors d'oeuvre, Taramosalata, which has crept into favour recently and certainly provides something uncommon. It is more properly made with dried roe of the grey mullet, but an anglicised version can be made with smoked cod's roe.

Pound the roe with fresh breadcrumbs, onion juice, lemon juice, pepper and olive oil until you have a smooth pâté-like consistence. Eat with plain hot toast or toast Melba.

COLD TRIPE

To many this may sound very odd indeed, but let me assure them that it is not. Wipe the cold cooked tripe and cut it into thin short strips. Mix with an ordinary oil-and-vinegar dressing with a touch of French mustard in it, and serve sprinkled with very finely chopped parsley and a little onion or shallot.

CUCUMBER WITH SOUR CREAM

As it is difficult if not impossible to sour one's fresh cream nowadays owing to pasteurisation of the milk, let me say that an admirable substitute called cultured cream can be obtained in many towns.

Peel the cucumbers, remove the centres and cut the flesh into little dice. Sprinkle them with salt and leave them for half an hour. Now pour away the liquid that has come from them and dress them with a mixture of pounded hard-

boiled egg-yolk seasoned with a little pepper, sour (cultured) cream and a very light dash of vinegar.

SMOKED SALMON AND CUCUMBER

Prepare the cucumber as in the recipe for cucumbers with sour cream (page 147) and mix with the little dice some short thin strips of fresh or tinned smoked salmon.

Dress lightly with lemon juice, pepper, just a touch of salt and olive oil made in the same way as an oil-and-vinegar dressing.

RED CABBAGE AND APPLE

Take some red cabbage out of its pickle, put it into a colander and run the cold tap over it.

Then drain it well, mix it with an equal quantity of peeled and cored dessert apple cut in short thin strips, and moisten with an ordinary French oil-and-vinegar dressing.

SPICED SALMON

Fresh salmon is too expensive to pickle nowadays, but this dish can conveniently be made with the best qualities of tinned salmon. Take a breakfastcupful of the best flakes and rinse them thoroughly (but very gently) with hot water, draining them very well afterwards and putting them in the serving dish.

Put a teacupful of good vinegar into a saucepan and add half a teaspoonful of whole cloves, half that quantity of whole allspice, four peppercorns and an eighth of a level teaspoonful of salt. Bring to the boil and pour over the salmon. Leave for two hours and serve the salmon flakes only on an hors d'oeuvre dish.

TOMATOES AND SWEET PEPPERS

Take equal quantities of ripe tomato and sweet red peppers, skin them, discard the centres and seeds of both and cut them into thin slices. Add to these two small onions, one shallot and some parsley all finely chopped, and dress at the last minute with oil-and-vinegar.

You can use tinned sweet peppers (pimientos) for this if you want to save trouble, but if you use the fresh ones they should be put under a slow grill for a short time until the skins can be peeled off, and of course allowed to grow cold before being added to the other ingredients.

TUNA FISH AND CELERY

Cut some drained tuna fish into small pieces and mix these with small pieces of the white part of raw celery.

Make a dressing of a little good vinegar into which you have mixed a little French mustard and the oil from the tin, and finish with chopped parsley and spring onion green. Mix and pour over the fish and celery.

Savouries and savoury butters

Savoury butters are served with grilled or fried fish and meat, usually in the form of round pats about an inch in diameter and a quarter to half an inch thick. They should normally be very cold, but some recipes demand that they should be half-melted. They are made by first creaming the butter and then mixing smoothly with it the other savoury ingredients required in the recipe. They are then spread out smoothly to the even thickness preferred, and after a stay in the refrigerator to chill the mixture well, it is cut into rounds of the desired size. The best-known of these butters is **maître d'hôtel butter,** which is made like this and is admirable with grilled or fried fish or with steaks and cutlets.

Mix with $\frac{1}{4}$ lb. creamed butter a dessertspoonful of finely chopped parsley, a little salt and pepper and a few drops of lemon juice.

Anchovy butter

Mix with $\frac{1}{4}$ lb. creamed butter as much anchovy essence, or better, anchovy paste, as your taste directs. Some like to add the yolk of a hard-boiled egg and a touch of lemon juice. I find myself that by far the best paste to use is the one called Gentleman's Relish.

Curry butter

Add to the creamed butter sufficient curry powder or paste to your taste.

Ham butter

Combine with $\frac{1}{4}$ lb. creamed butter, the same amount of pounded lean cooked ham and two hard-boiled egg-yolks.

Garlic butter

Add as much pounded garlic, or garlic juice as your taste dictates.

Mustard butter

Mix with the creamed butter French mustard or made English mustard to your taste.

Paprika butter

Mix with $\frac{1}{4}$ lb. creamed butter a small teaspoonful of paprika pepper, moistening with a few drops of white wine or consommé.

Sardine butter

Pound an equal quantity of skinned and boned sardines, well drained from the oil in the tin, with $\frac{1}{4}$ lb. creamed butter, seasoning with a little cayenne pepper. Finely chopped parsley can also be added if liked and some fancy a very small teaspoonful of tinned tomato paste or tomato sauce.

Shrimp butter

Add to the creamed butter an equal quantity of pounded picked shrimps or shrimp paste to taste. Heighten the flavour with a touch of lemon juice.

Soft roe butter

Add to $\frac{1}{4}$ lb. creamed butter the same weight either of tinned soft herrings' roes or fresh roes

149

first poached in a buttered pan with the juice of half a lemon and well drained. Mix in also a small teaspoonful of made mustard.

Tomato butter

The simplest way to make this is to mix with the creamed butter as much tinned tomato paste as your palate prefers. A little minced parsley might also be added.

Watercress butter

Make just as maître d'hôtel butter, using finely minced watercress instead of parsley.

Note: All these butters will, of course, be finer if after mixing they are passed through a sieve.

HOT LIVER PÂTÉ

We are so used to cold pâtés nowadays that we have forgotten how nice they can be when served hot.

1 lb. calf's liver in one piece : 1 breakfastcupful of breadcrumbs : 2 teaspoonfuls each of grated onion and chopped parsley : a teaspoonful of finely minced celery : salt and pepper : 2 eggs : ½ pint milk.

Pour boiling water over the piece of liver, leave for five minutes and then drain, cut it up and put through a mincer. Add the breadcrumbs and seasonings with salt and pepper, mix well together and bind with the egg beaten into the milk.

Pack the mixture tightly into a buttered cake-tin and bake in a slow oven until the pâté is firm, which will take about an hour. Turn out to serve with a suitable sauce or gravy poured over it and braised onions and boiled new potatoes to accompany it. This can of course be pressed, allowed to become cold and served sliced with hot toast.

BEEF MARROW TOAST

This is said to have been one of the favourite savouries of Queen Victoria. It is certainly delicious but extremely rich, and it must be served very hot indeed. An early twentieth century cookery book gives this recipe which in my opinion cannot be beaten.

Get the butcher to crack the marrow bones so that you can get the marrow out, and let this soak in cold water, changing the water once or twice. Then drop it into a pan of boiling water for five or six minutes. It will look yellowish when done.

Drain it in a colander, then cut it in slices or pieces and put it on slightly buttered toast. Season with salt and pepper and put the toasts into the oven just to heat and soften the marrow. The toasts themselves should not get crisp.

SAVOURY STUFFED APPLES

6 cooking apples : 1 teacupful sage and onion stuffing (Volume One, page 66) : 2 teaspoonfuls of butter : salt and pepper.

Paté

Peel and core the fair-sized apples, season the stuffing with salt and pepper and fill the cavities with it. Put the butter in a shallow pie-dish with three tablespoonfuls of water and let it get hot in the oven. Then put in the stuffed apples with a small flake of butter on top of each, and bake slowly until cooked, about half an hour.

These apples make a particularly good garnish for pork chops.

SCOTCH WOODCOCK

The modern version of this admirable savoury is to spread some hot buttered toasts with anchovy paste and to surmount this by a nice heap of buttered egg, page 81. This is criss-crossed on top with thin strips of hot anchovy fillets, and a caper is placed in each interstice. A pinch of chopped or minced parsley completes it.

An older version of the savoury, however, is as follows. Make some thick, crustless buttered toast and spread this with the anchovy paste. Pile the toast in three layers on a dish, and pour over it a thick custard made with three eggs and a little cream. This is really much the same but presented in a different manner.

To my own taste the anchovy paste known as Gentleman's Relish is far better for this dish than the ordinary paste of that name.

Fish

The fish repertory of the British kitchen is wide and excellent, and a great number of our dishes may rightly take pride of place in any well-ordered meal. The simpler dishes like jellied eels or cold fried fish are not out of place in any cold collation, even if their origins are humble in the extreme, and our own less sophisticated version of the Russian fish pie, the pickled halibut, the herring and mackerel recipes and the smoked haddock balls are admirable substitutes for those richer and more complicated dishes introduced to us from the Continent.

Nevertheless, in order to follow the food conventions of the day some of these must be mentioned, particularly for crab, lobster, red mullet and scallops, and some of the less demanding will be found here. I would like specially to recommend the really regal smoked salmon tart which though French in origin will bring a comparatively inexpensive touch of luxury to any meal with which it is served.

COD AND MUSHROOMS ON SKEWERS

Cut some cod fillets into small squares and alternate them on skewers with small mushrooms. Sprinkle with salt and pepper, dust with flour and then brush over with beaten egg and roll in breadcrumbs.

Fry quickly all over in shallow butter and serve either with a hot horseradish sauce (Volume One, page 28), or with tomato sauce and a white risotto (page 194).

COD STEAKS

This way of serving fried cod steaks not only gives them the unfamiliar taste of olive oil, but a pleasant garnish as well which is not too difficult for a modest dinner party.

Small steaks from the tail end are best for this, but if unobtainable, pieces of fillet about the same size could be used instead.

Dip them into a mixture of flour, salt and pepper and brown them lightly on both sides in shallow olive oil. Arrange them on a thick bed of stewed or tinned tomatoes, cooked until quite thick and not at all watery. Garnish them with little dice of fried potato and small mushrooms, both cooked in olive oil, and crisp rings of onion fried in deep fat, these to be in alternate mounds round the dish. A sprinkling of coarsely chopped parsley completes a savoury and colourful dish.

MOCK CRAB

A Victorian dish to console those unable at the right moment to get a real crab.

1 ½ lb. very finely shredded cooked cod : ¼ pint white vinegar flavoured with anchovy essence : 2 tablespoonfuls made mustard : 1 tablespoonful salad oil : 4 tablespoonfuls grated cheese : green salad : mayonnaise sauce.

Flake up the fish finely with two forks so as to resemble crab flesh, put into a bowl and season with salt and white pepper. Now in a separate basin mix well together the vinegar, mustard and salad oil, and when well amalgamated moisten the fish with it. Lastly sprinkle the grated cheese over it (Parmesan cheese is best here) and toss the mixture together.

Heap up in a bed of lettuce and hand some mayonnaise sauce with it.

CURRIED CRAB

2 medium-sized cooked crabs : $\frac{1}{4}$ pint curry sauce (page 193) : 1 tablespoonful cream : lemon.

Remove the flesh from the body and claws of the crabs, and heat them in the curry sauce. When hot, add the cream and lemon juice to taste and serve in a border of plainly boiled rice.

SCRAMBLED CRAB

1 cooked crab : 1 oz. butter : $\frac{1}{4}$ pint milk : 5 eggs : $\frac{1}{2}$ teaspoonful chopped parsley : salt, pepper and cayenne pepper : lemon.

Heat the milk, butter and seasoning to taste and mix the flaked crab with this.

Beat the eggs lightly, add them to the crab mixture and stir until the scramble is thick enough. Then stir in the parsley and cayenne pepper, finish with a drop or two of lemon juice and serve in a border of plainly boiled rice or on toasts as a savoury or supper dish.

JELLIED EELS

A traditionally popular dish with great numbers of the English public and by no means to be despised in its own right, if you can bring your-self to deal with this slippery customer.

2 lb. skinned eels : 2 onions : 2 medium carrots : a small bunch of parsley, thyme and bay leaf : 1 doz. black peppercorns. The eels should be cut into two-inch lengths, which the fish-monger will no doubt do for you, as well as skinning them.

Cut the vegetables in slices and put them into a saucepan with the herbs. Add the pieces of eel on top of them and just cover with cold water, salting this a little and adding the peppercorns. Bring to the boil very slowly, put on the lid and simmer gently for an hour or so until the pieces are tender.

Take them out and put them in a deep dish, and reduce the cooking liquor by rapid boiling until you have two-thirds left. Strain this over the eels and leave in a cool place where the liquid will eventually set in a jelly.

COLD FRIED FISH

Cold fried fish is much appreciated by those who know of it, but it must be fried in a special way.

Oil should be used and the cooking done, not in deep oil, but in a frying-pan.

Flour the fillets with seasoned flour, and then dip them in beaten egg. Get the oil very hot and fry the fillets in it on each side, putting in the skin side first, which will prevent the fillet from curling up.

153

Drain the golden-brown fillets on kitchen paper, and eat when absolutely cold. Plaice is a particularly good fish for this dish, I think.

FISH TART (TOURTE DE POISSON)

This is one of those superfine fish dishes which one always hopes for yet never expects to get. Once again, the only difficulty about it is the trouble its preparation takes.

First of all make a flan case with your best and most suitable pastry and bake it blind. Set this aside while you cook some noodles (page 197), drain them and bind them with cream. Poach also some small slices of fillet of sole and of turbot (and if you can, of John Dory) either in salted water or in a mixture of water and dry white wine.

Make a sauce of this with some cooking liquor from mussels and from mushrooms (see below) and thicken and enrich it with egg-yolk beaten with a little cream. Mix with the pieces of fish.

Fill the flan case with this mixed with the noodles, sprinkle with grated Gruyère cheese, and brown quickly just before serving.

If desired, the button mushrooms and the mussels themselves, with any black parts removed, could be included in the filling, and if quantity is the object so could be some fish forcemeat (page 66) shaped into small meringue-shaped quenelles with two teaspoons and then poached and well drained.

But it is best just with the noodles, the pieces of fish and the delicious sauce with which they are bound together.

Mushroom cooking liquor

This is the juice which comes from stewing mushrooms in butter, and should always be kept for flavouring.

Mussels

Mussels cooking liquor is obtained from cooking mussels in this way. To a pint and a half of mussels, well scraped and brushed, add half a medium-sized onion and half a shallot finely chopped, two or three parsley stalks, a small sprig of thyme, a quarter of a small bay leaf, a small pinch of freshly-ground pepper and four tablespoonfuls of dry white wine. Cover the pan tightly, put it on a quick heat and after two minutes give it a good shake. Do this two or three more times during the cooking, which should not take more than five or six minutes in all.

The mussels should by then be cooked and their shells wide open. In case of the presence of any sand, the liquid should be decanted through a fine cloth before being used for the sauce.

If they are to be included in the tart, the mussels should of course be taken from their shells. The mushrooms for this purpose should be very small button ones, kept white during their cooking.

SMOKED HADDOCK BALLS

Ordinary fish cakes are always popular, but this sort are unusual—and unusually nice.

Flake up finely some cooked smoked haddock, mix with butter to taste, plenty of freshly-ground black pepper and a little cream, and then mix with an equal quantity of mashed potato.

Shape in smallish balls, golf-ball size, with floured hands, egg-and-breadcrumb, and fry in deep fat or oil.

You could serve a hot mayonnaise sauce with them if you are adventurous. This is made by mixing mayonnaise sauce with Béchamel sauce (Volume One, page 22) or other white sauce until you have the flavour you like.

HALIBUT WITH TOMATOES AND PEPPERS

Devotees of sweet green peppers will appreciate this pleasant way of using them to enhance the flavour of a pleasant fish.

1½ lb. piece of halibut : 3 tomatoes : 1 green sweet pepper.

Butter a shallow fireproof dish and lay the piece of halibut in it. Sprinkle this with salt and pepper and arrange over the top five or six thick slices of skinned tomato and very thin strips of the green pepper from which you have first removed midribs and seeds. Bake in a hot oven for half an hour, basting it frequently with the liquid in the dish.

PICKLED HALIBUT

An interesting and unusual way with this fish, which is excellent for a fish salad or even as an hors d'oeuvre.

1 lb. cooked halibut : ½ pint good vinegar : cayenne pepper : mace.

Put the halibut into a bowl and pour over it the hot vinegar which you have first boiled for twenty minutes or so with a blade of mace and a fraction of cayenne pepper, but be careful here, only a fraction ! Let it stand in the cold for two days before serving.

HERRINGS IN A CRUST

Roll out some short-crust pastry an eighth of an inch thick, and cut in pieces the length and breadth of a herring.

Fillet the herrings, and after seasoning the inside of the fillets put every pair together to counterfeit the whole fish. Lay these on the pieces of short crust and cover with a few flakes of butter and some minced chives or onion green. Cover with another piece of the paste, pinch the edges well together and bake in a moderate oven for twenty minutes to half an hour according to the size of the fish.

Hand a hot horseradish sauce with them.

JOHN DORY WITH ASPARAGUS

It was at the latter end of the nineteenth century that English cooks first learned to appreciate the 155

Lobster Mornay

ugly John Dory, and found that when filleted it can be treated in many of the same ways as sole. Here is one.

Buy smallish fish and have the fishmonger fillet them.

Season and flour them and fry them golden on each side in a little butter. When cooked, dish them and garnish with cooked or tinned or frozen asparagus tips warmed in a little butter.

Sprinkle grated cheese over all, and brown quickly under the grill.

LOBSTER

Two lobster dishes which have been steadily gaining in popularity for star performance on a party occasion are the following. It is true that lobsters are expensive, but the Mornay version at any rate can be made with crab, crayfish tails or the ubiquitous scampi instead.

LOBSTER MORNAY

Lobster (cooked) : cheese sauce (see page 22).

Cut the flesh from the lobster's tail and claws into neat pieces, keeping the two halves of the tail intact. In the bottom of the shells spread a few spoonfuls of the cheese sauce, and then arrange the pieces of lobster on top. Cover with more cheese sauce and sprinkle with grated cheese. Brown in the oven or under the grill.

LOBSTER NEWBURG

Lobster (cooked) : $\frac{3}{4}$ pint cream : sherry or Madeira : 1 egg-yolk.

Cut the flesh from a medium-sized lobster in suitable pieces and put them into a well-buttered shallow pan. Season them well with salt and pepper and a touch of cayenne, and heat them on both sides until the outside membranes turn a fine red colour. Now almost cover them with the wine and boil this away until there is practically nothing left, perhaps a teaspoonful. Now pour over the pieces the cream into which you have first beaten the egg-yolk, and shake or stir very gently until this rich sauce thickens. Serve in a border of plainly boiled rice.

BUTTERED LOBSTER

The very simplest way of eating a lobster hot is by buttering it in this very old English way. It is the nearest approach to enjoying a hot freshly boiled lobster with lashings of melted butter, and has the advantage of being made with lobster already cooked.

Just remove the flesh from the shell and claws of a cold boiled lobster and toss them, without cooking them any more, in a little melted butter until just heated through. Black freshly ground pepper is demanded here, I think, and a little sprinkling of lemon juice and chopped parsley may be permitted, but the flavours of the lobster and the butter are all that is really needed.

LOBSTER CUTLETS

One of the very best kind of fishcakes there are. They used to be much enjoyed in my youth at the Mitre at Hampton Court followed by roast duck and green peas and then a small apple pie for each person, a truly English meal.

1 cooked lobster : 1 oz. flour : 1 tablespoonful cream : 1 oz. butter : $\frac{1}{4}$ pint fish stock in which the lobster shells should have played their part.

Make a thick panada (see page 25, Volume One) with the butter, flour and stock, give it a good boil and then add the cream. Season with salt, pepper and a touch of cayenne and then stir in the flesh from the lobster cut in small dice. Mix well, turn out on to a buttered plate and smooth flat and cover with a piece of buttered greaseproof paper or kitchen foil. When cold, shape into cutlets with floured hands, egg-and-breadcrumb these and fry in deep fat. A little piece of the small legs of the lobster or of the feelers may be inserted at the end of each cutlet after frying, to counterfeit the cutlet's bone.

Serve garnished with fried parsley (see page 204).

DEVILLED LOBSTER

1 large cooked lobster : 3 tablespoonfuls breadcrumbs : a few browned breadcrumbs : 1½ oz. butter : 2 tablespoonfuls cream : salt, pepper and cayenne pepper.

Cut the lobster in half lengthways, remove the flesh from the two half-shells and chop it up finely. Pour the melted butter over this and then mix in the breadcrumbs, and the cream, seasoning rather highly with the cayenne pepper.

Press the mixture lightly into each half-shell, sprinkle with the browned breadcrumbs and arrange a few flakes of butter on top, and bake for about twenty minutes in a moderate oven.

Some have been known to eat this cold when on a picnic, but it is vastly preferable when hot.

LOBSTER PANCAKES

A really high-class dinner-party or light luncheon dish, which actually can cost very little.

Lobster : ½ pint Béchamel or white sauce (see Volume One, page 22) : 1–2 tablespoonfuls tomato purée : paprika pepper : thin unsweetened pancakes.

The lobster, a small one, can be cooked, frozen or tinned or prawns or scampi can be substituted.

Cut the shellfish into small pieces, season them with salt and pepper and a little paprika pepper (for colour) and toss them in a little butter. Bind them with a little of the sauce which you have flavoured to your taste with the tomato purée and spread a little of this on each pancake, which can have been cooked previously if desired. Roll each up and lay them side by side in a long fireproof dish and cover them with more of the plain white sauce. Sprinkle with grated cheese if you like, and brown quickly under the grill.

GRILLED MACKEREL

An American fashion from Cape Cod which is rapidly becoming naturalised by garlic addicts.

Rub a bowl round with a cut clove of garlic and in it mix a tablespoonful of olive oil with a little salt and pepper.

Split a mackerel open and rub this flavoured oil on it inside and out, and then grill the fish until well browned on each side.

Serve with lemon juice and melted butter sprinkled over it.

PRAWN COCKTAIL

Although this is an American speciality which can be made as well with shrimps, lobster, crab or other suitable fish, it has been firmly adopted in this country in recent years.

Small glasses are first lined with lettuce leaves

and the cooked, tinned or frozen prawns are put inside it. A generous spoonful of the following cocktail sauce is poured over them and they are served as cold as possible.

Cocktail sauce

1 teacupful chilli sauce: 3 teaspoonfuls white vinegar: 6 drops Tabasco sauce: 1 level teaspoonful celery salt: $\frac{1}{2}$ level teaspoonful each salt and dry mustard: $\frac{1}{4}$ level teaspoonful pepper: 2 teaspoonfuls Worcestershire sauce: 1 level teaspoonful each of grated onion and finely minced parsley and if you like, 1 level teaspoonful of grated horseradish.

GRILLED RED MULLET

This pretty little fish is particularly enjoyed by the epicure who insists that the liver should be left inside it when cleaned, some even contend-

Prawn cocktail

159

ing that the fish should not be cleaned at all. However you may like it, grilling is certainly one of the best ways of cooking it.

1 red mullet for each person : lemon : parsley : olive oil : half-melted maître d'hôtel butter.

Score the fish three or four times diagonally on each side, season it all over with salt and pepper and put it into a shallow dish. Put a few slices of lemon on top with some broken parsley stalks and sprinkle it with lemon juice and a little olive oil. Leave it thus for an hour or so, turning it over now and then.

When wanted, grill it on both sides under a rather hot grill, sprinkling it now and then with the liquid in which it has been lying. It will take about twenty minutes. Serve at once with a little half-melted maître d'hôtel butter, that is, butter kneaded with chopped parsley and lemon juice.

RED MULLET NIÇOISE

This simple dish looks extremely exotic in the South of France, but finds its way to many modest tables in this country today.

Red Mullet : tomatoes : garlic : anchovy fillets in oil : black or green olives : butter : anchovy essence.

The red mullet are grilled in the usual way (Volume One, page 30) and they are served with a thick purée of tomatoes poured over them and a decoration of anchovies and stoned olives cut in strips. Anchovy butter should be handed with them.

The tomato purée is made by stewing ripe tomatoes, cut up but with their skins on, in a dessertspoonful of olive oil with a chopped clove of garlic for twenty minutes. This is then rubbed through a sieve, and cooked on until the right thickness is obtained.

The anchovy butter is made by kneading anchovy paste or essence to taste with a good piece of butter, which after a short stay in the refrigerator is cut into round pats and handed separately.

SALMON IN ASPIC

Devotees of this noble dish are often divided in opinion as to whether the fish should be cooked (as I myself contend) in plain salt and water or in what the French call a court-bouillon. There is something to be said for the latter if the fish is to be eaten cold, as it will have gained extra flavour by being left in the cooking liquor while it cools, but all things being equal the times for boiling it are those given on page 29 of Volume One.

The salmon shown in the illustration on page 161 has been cooked in this way, and when cold the skin of the upper side has been removed. It was then decorated in the manner shown, with cucumber, black olives (instead of truffle), prawns, parsley and stuffed olive. The surround of the dish was garnished with lemon, red sweet peppers and so on.

The flavour of the fish will no doubt be all that

can be expected, in whatever liquid it has been cooked, but its gastronomical value has been enhanced by the attraction of the decoration that has been devised for it. Such a decoration, as also in the case of hams or gammons of bacon, of mousses or chaudfroid of chicken which will be found in these pages, helps to promote the appetite of the eager diner to the credit of the decorator's ingenuity. It affords a lesson which can be applied in the presentation of all cold dishes, but never of hot ones, the deliciousness of which will be impaired if they have to be kept waiting while the decoration is applied.

COURT-BOUILLON FOR SALMON

Proportions : 3 quarts water : 2 oz. coarse salt : not quite $\frac{1}{4}$ pint vinegar : 3 oz. carrot and 3 oz. onion both cut in round slices : $\frac{1}{2}$ oz. parsley stalks : $\frac{1}{2}$ bay leaf : 1 sprig of thyme : not quite $\frac{1}{2}$ oz. coarsely ground peppercorns.

Bring to the boil and boil gently for three-quarters of an hour. Strain and leave to get cold.

SALMON CUTLETS

Salmon is usually so expensive that we are glad to make the most of it when we can. So instead of serving it in steaks, try this excellent way instead, which preserves all the flavour of the fresh fish.

Chop up some raw salmon with a knife, rather coarsely, and measure out a quarter of its weight of breadcrumbs first soaked in creamy milk or cream and then squeezed as dry as possible. Go on chopping all together until you get a well-mixed paste, seasoning with salt and pepper. Spread this out on a floured board about half an inch thick, smooth it evenly and cut it into cutlet shapes. Do this just before you want to cook them and, if you are wise, let the mixture chill a little in the refrigerator before you do so.

Fry them golden on each side in butter and if 161

you like hand some creamily stewed mushrooms with them.

SALMON MOUSSE

First line a china soufflé mould with aspic jelly, and when it is set arrange a decoration of cucumber or cooked green peas or peas and pea-shaped carrot in the bottom. (This lining is best done with the aspic in a half-melted condition, and the mould should previously have been well chilled.)

Meanwhile you will have made the mousse by reducing some cooked salmon flesh to a purée, by sieving or other mechanical means, and to this you must add white sauce made with fish stock, half-whipped double cream and aspic jelly in the proportions of a quarter of a pint of the sauce, the same of the cream and a couple of good tablespoonfuls of aspic jelly to each pound of the salmon purée. Taste for seasoning which should be very delicate and if you think it looks a bit pallid, stir in a drop or two of carmine colouring.

Salmon mousse

When well set and chilled, turn out so that the cucumber or green pea garnish (or any other decoration for prettiness you may have thought of) is shown at the top.

FRIED SALMON

This cavalier treatment of the much esteemed salmon may shock some people, but it is really very good, my early twentieth century Scotswoman contending that it is a fine dish for breakfast.

Cut the salmon into not too thin cutlets, right across the fish and for this purpose cutting slant-wise towards the tail end not straight down. Leave on the skin and dip both sides in beaten egg, dusting them after this with flour or fine oatmeal. Fry them, one side after the other, in hot oil, which will take about a quarter of an hour altogether.

No seasoning is used and no sauce is handed with them.

SMOKED SALMON TART

We usually eat our smoked salmon as an hors d'oeuvre, with cut lemon and brown bread-and-butter, but this is a very far superior way of enjoying this attractive smoked fish.

Line a sponge-tin with short pastry, and beat up lightly four whole eggs and two yolks, just enough to mix them together as for an omelette. Mix them with three-quarters of a pint of cream, season with salt, pepper and nutmeg and put this mixture into the flan case.

Sprinkle over the top a few small flakes of butter and then cover the filling completely with very thin slices of smoked salmon. Bake in a hot oven for thirty-five minutes, until the filling is set and the edges of the slices faintly showing through. Serve at once, as delay may cause the salmon to get tough.

SCALLOPS

For both these dishes the scallops are used raw, which is something unusual for British cooks.

Fried scallops

Cut the white part of the scallops into rounds, so that you have two or three, according to thickness, where there was only one before, but leave the orange parts whole. Season with salt and pepper, roll lightly in flour and egg-and-breadcrumb them. Fry golden on each side in shallow butter. Hand tomato sauce with them.

Grilled scallops en brochette

Cut the white part in pieces and leave the orange parts whole or, if very large, in halves, and im-pale them on long skewers, one for each person, alternately with small squares of thinnish streaky green bacon or blanched pickled pork. Season them with salt and pepper, baste them with melted butter and cook under the grill for about a quarter of an hour, until the edges of the bacon

Sole en goujons

are slightly burnt. Small cubes of mushrooms can also be alternated if wished, but nothing else. Hand a Hollandaise sauce with them, for which see Volume One, page 25.

FRIED STRIPS OF SOLE

A habit which we have adopted from France in recent years is both economical (since it tends to make the fish go further) and attractive by its unfamiliarity. This is what the French call presenting fishes like sole, lemon sole, plaice, etc. en goujons, which is done by cutting the fillets diagonally in strips about the size of a small sardine. The little river fish, the gudgeon, after which this dish is named, is seldom seen in the home in this country, but the sardine simile is well enough.

The sole fillets having been cut up thus are generally egg-and-breadcrumbed and fried in deep fat or oil and then served in a crisp and golden heap often with Tartare sauce (page 26,

Volume One) handed with them. Or they may be dipped in fritter batter and then fried in the same way, but the egg-and-breadcrumb manner is the better, I think.

The knowledgeable will also add a garnish of fried parsley (page 204).

BAKED SPRATS

These sometimes despised little fish, which are really excellent, can make quite an elegant dish if presented in this way.

Clean them and wipe them dry and arrange them side by side and head to tail in a long buttered fireproof dish in which they will be served. Season with salt and pepper and sprinkle a little finely chopped parsley. Bake in a moderate oven for about twenty minutes, and on serving sprinkle with lemon juice. If you like you could sprinkle their insides after cleaning with a little mixed spice.

If they are liked spicy, they can appear as

soused sprats as a cold dish, cooked in the same way as soused herring or mackerel. Their diminutive size makes them more appetising too.

GRILLED TROUT

This is the Highland fashion. The oatmeal gives the fish a particularly nutty flavour.

Dust each trout with salt, but no pepper. Roll them in fine oatmeal, and grill them carefully on a well-buttered or oiled grill.

Six to eight minutes should do the trick.

TROUT WITH ALMONDS

The French have long cooked their small trout, one for each person, in the fashion called à la meunière, but the Americans have evolved a variation of this which has become a favourite here.

Season the little trout, flour them and fry them golden on both sides in butter. Transfer them to the serving dish, and add a little more butter to the frying-pan, cooking on until it is a light brown and nutty-smelling. Pour this over the fish and sprinkle them with chopped parsley and lemon juice, and add at the last some long thin strips of blanched almonds which have previously been lightly browned in butter.

Trout and almonds

TURBOT WITH CUCUMBER

Fillets or steaks of turbot, as cut for grilling, can be used here.

Turbot steaks : butter : parsley : lemon : cucumber.

Roll the fish in flour seasoned with salt and pepper and fry them golden on each side in a little shallow butter. When they are done, put them aside, add a little more butter to that in the frying-pan and go on cooking it until it browns very lightly. Then add a sprinkle of chopped parsley and a squeeze of lemon juice and pour over the fish, serving them with a garnish of olive-shaped pieces of cucumber (no peel) which you have first stewed in butter.

RUSSIAN FISH PIE

Fish pie usually denotes a mashed potato covering, but there is a much nicer version with a pastry lid which is quite suitable for party occasions.

Flaky pastry made with $\frac{1}{2}$ lb. flour: $\frac{3}{4}$ lb. roughly flaked cooked white fish : 1 hard-boiled egg : 1 teaspoonful chopped parsley : 2 tablespoonfuls white sauce : 1 lemon : eight tinned or bottled mushrooms.

Mix together the fish, parsley, chopped egg, grated lemon rind to taste, the white sauce and the mushrooms cut in small pieces. Roll the pastry into a square about a quarter of an inch thick and put the fish mixture into the middle. Brush the edges of the pastry with beaten egg and gather the corners to the middle, closing the joins tightly together and brushing the whole thing over with beaten egg. Bake in a hot oven for about three-quarters of an hour until the pastry is cooked.

Some whole picked shrimps or even oysters may be added to the mixture if liked.

Meat

Indigenous meat dishes are none too exciting, though when beautifully cooked and presented they carry their own recommendation. In this section I have chosen a small selection of the kind of dishes which the cook-hostess might prefer to choose for the special delectation of her guests: the present popular beef steaks Diane, the peppery au poivre and the uncooked and highly masculine steak Tartare; such dishes as the Russian boeuf Stroganoff, the French version of stewed tripe, the Italian of knuckle of veal; the Swedish pork with prunes; the monumental sausages with cabbage. Those who like to cook with wine or beer will find recipes for chicken with the former and wood pigeons or sausages with the latter, and those who wish to profit from the American gastronomical invasion of the past few years will discover their versions of cooking chickens or ham or gammon of bacon to whet their appetites for further investigation. The more economically-minded are directed to ways of stuffing mutton chops to make them go further, to the art of serving the kebab and to the delights of cooking the meat hedgehog, the delicious and now almost unknown giblet pie, and to the mysteries of kidney embalmed in a baked potato.

BEEF STEAK

Two interesting ways of varying the plain beef steak have of recent years been borrowed from the French kitchen and are highly popular with diners-out, most of whom, however, do not know how easily these dishes can be made.

Pepper steak (steak au poivre)

First of all take some black peppercorns and crush them on a board with the bottom of a heavy pan or a flat iron, until you have a very coarse powder. Have your beef steak ready, salt it on both sides and then coat it all over with the coarse pepper crushings, beating it so that it is well incorporated into the meat. Now heat some butter and olive oil, half and half, in a heavy frying-pan and when it is very hot indeed, almost smoking, put in the steak and fry it first on one side and then the other until it reaches the state of 'done-ness' that you want. Put it on a plate, and pour off the fat in the pan. Put the steak back in the pan again and pour a liqueur glassful of brandy over it. Set this alight, and when the flames have died down, put the steak on the serving dish. Pour a little beef gravy into the pan with a teaspoonful of cream and, stirring and scraping the bottom of the pan with a wooden spoon, let this mixture thicken a little. Take the pan from the heat, season with a little salt, and stir in a few small bits of butter, shaking the pan as you do so. Pour this delicious sauce over the steak and serve with sauté potatoes.

Steak Diane

Beat the steak until flat. Fry a chopped shallot 167

or small onion in butter until golden, then fry the seasoned steak quietly until done as you like it, on both sides. Add a few drops of Worcester-shire sauce, pour a liqueurglassful of brandy over, and set it alight.

Serve sprinkled with chopped parsley and accompanied by some sort of fried potato.

CUMBERLAND BEEF STEAKS
Savoury steak

Rump steak: 1 teacupful good vinegar: 1 tea-spoonful salt: $\frac{1}{2}$ teaspoonful pepper: 3 tea-spoonfuls brown sugar: 1 teaspoonful chopped parsley: 1 teacupful ketchup.

Mix the ingredients together, pour them into a deep dish and let the steak soak in them for twelve hours, turning it over now and then.

When wanted, drain the steak well, dredge it lightly with flour and grill it. Meanwhile make a thick sauce with the liquid in which it was soak-ing, and serve with fried potatoes.

Stuffed steak

Get a large piece of steak, about two pounds in weight, beat it and then rub it with a little butter. Now make a sage-and-onion stuffing (Volume One, page 66) adding to it a little chopped bacon.

Spread this on the steak, roll it up and tie it tightly with string and bake in a deep covered dish in a moderate oven for two hours, basting frequently with dripping as it cooks. Eat hot or cold.

BEEF TOURNEDOS

A Tournedos is a round slice from the best part of the fillet of beef, cut about an inch thick and weighing roughly six ounces. It is fried or grilled in the same way as any steak, save that this must be done very quickly to ensure its absolute tenderness. It is usually served on a round of fried bread of the same size, and is garnished in a large number of ways, of which the following are a few:

Tournedos Alsacienne: grilled bacon and sauerkraut (choucroûte).

Béarnaise: with the sauce of that name handed separately.

Catalane: on artichoke bottoms instead of fried bread, surrounded by grilled tomatoes, with thickened gravy handed separately.

Continentale: with grilled mushrooms and tomatoes, sprigs of watercress, thick fried po-tatoes and maître d'hôtel butter handed separately.

Niçoise: the bread is fried in olive oil instead of butter, the garnish is of baked tomato-halves stuffed with breadcrumbs, parsley and garlic, each tournedos being surmounted by a curled anchovy fillet: surround with tomato sauce.

Rossini: the tournedos is surmounted by a slice of foie gras and masked with Madeira sauce (which nowadays can very conveniently be bought in small tins).

PORTMANTEAU STEAK

A highly masculine Victorian dish of exquisite flavour. In these less generous days the small Cornish oysters from Helford River are just right for it.

Have a nice beef steak cut from the rump or fillet about an inch and a half thick. Cut a deep pocket in one side of it horizontally, and into this stuff half a dozen oysters dusted with a little pepper. Fry the steak in the usual way after sewing up the pocket with cotton, and when ready serve at once with its own delicious gravy and one or two pats of butter very lightly flavoured with anchovy on top. Garnish with a few sprigs of watercress.

BEEF STEAK MIRABEAU

In the old days anchovies were often used to give a different salt taste in stews of meat and were quite a feature of British cooking. Today the same combination makes this kind of steak acceptable and unusual.

Fry the steak in the usual way, and when it is done, criss-cross the top with very thin warmed strips of anchovy fillets and place in each square half a stoned or stuffed green olive.

BEEF OLIVES

1 lb. good beef steak : 2 oz. savoury forcemeat : braising vegetables or 1 pint good stock : 1 oz. butter and 1 oz. flour for thickening.

Cut the steak into quarter-inch thick slices, beat these and cut into rectangular pieces about three inches long by two and a half inches wide. Sprinkle each of these very lightly with salt and pepper and spread thinly with some of the force-meat, rolling them up and either tying them with cotton or transfixing with cocktail sticks.

Braise them or stew them for about an hour and a half, then remove the cotton or sticks and serve them garnished with grilled tomatoes and potato rissoles. Thicken the cooking liquid with the butter and flour and pour this over the little rolls.

This dish has really nothing to do with olives as such but I suppose was given the name because the little rolls slightly resemble large Spanish olives in shape and size. As a matter of fact my mother used to include a few sliced olives in the thickened gravy and we always thought them rather nice.

BEEF GOULASH

Paprika pepper has become a familiar taste in the British kitchen today and here is a good way of using it.

$1\frac{1}{2}$ lb. beef steak : 2 oz. lard : 4 oz. onions : $\frac{1}{2}$ teaspoonful salt : paprika pepper to taste : $\frac{1}{2}$ lb. tomatoes : $\frac{1}{2}$ lb. smallish potatoes : 2 tablespoons sour cream.

Cut the steak into one-inch cubes and fry these in the lard with the roughly chopped onions until the latter are golden. Then add the

169

salt and not less than half a teaspoonful of the paprika pepper. Now add the tomatoes peeled and quartered and a teacupful of water, cover the pan and cook for an hour and a half in a moderate oven. Then add the potatoes cut in quarters, with another teacupful of water and cover and cook again in the same way for another hour, when the potatoes should be done and the liquid almost entirely absorbed. Add the sour cream if it is being used about ten minutes before serving.

BOEUF BOURGUIGNONNE

A magnificent dish for a special occasion.

$2\frac{1}{2}$ lb. chuck or buttock steak : some seasoned flour and $\frac{1}{2}$ oz. of unseasoned flour: $2\frac{1}{2}$ oz. butter : 2 tablespoons oil : 5 tablespoons brandy : 4 oz. bacon : 4 oz. button onions : 1 crushed clove of garlic : 1 tablespoon tomato purée : $\frac{3}{4}$ pint red wine : water : salt and pepper : 4 oz. button mushrooms : 1 dessertspoon sugar : 2 tablespoons chopped parsley.

Cut the meat into large cubes and roll them in the seasoned flour. Using 2 oz. of the butter and the oil, fry the meat all over in a large frying-pan until brown, then add the brandy and ignite. When the flame dies out transfer the meat to a casserole. Fry the bacon, onions and garlic until golden brown and put them in

Boeuf Bourguignonne

with the meat. Add the tomato purée, the mushrooms and the wine, and enough water to just cover the meat. Add salt and pepper. Cook in a moderate oven, 325° F or Regulo 3 for $2\frac{1}{4}$ hours.

Cream the remaining $\frac{1}{2}$ oz. of butter and the unseasoned flour together (this is known as Beurre Manie) and whisk into the casserole and cook for a further threequarters of an hour.

As a final touch add the sugar and chopped parsley. Adjust the seasoning if necessary.

BOEUF STROGANOFF

Russian dishes have always been a matter of curiosity in this country, though few of us know anything about them save caviare, which is far too expensive to buy for regular use. But those who like the flavour of sour or cultured cream may like to try this.

$1\frac{1}{2}$ lb. fillet of beef : 2 onions : $\frac{1}{4}$ lb. mushrooms : 4 oz. butter : 1 tablespoonful flour : 1 tablespoonful tomato purée : 1 teaspoonful made mustard : $\frac{1}{2}$ pint meat stock : $\frac{1}{4}$ pint sour or cultured cream : 1 teaspoonful salt : $\frac{1}{2}$ teaspoonful pepper : 1 tablespoonful chopped parsley.

Two hours before you want to cook the dish, cut the meat into strips about an inch long and a quarter of an inch thick, sprinkle them with salt and pepper and leave them to stand. When ready to start cooking, fry the sliced onion in the butter, add the sliced mushrooms and fry to-gether for two or three minutes. Then add the meat strips and fry all together for another five or six minutes, tossing with a fork. Sprinkle in the flour, fry another two or three minutes and then stir in the tomato purée and the mustard. Now dilute smoothly with the stock, add the sour cream, put on the lid and simmer gently for a quarter of an hour. When ready to serve, give it a boil up and serve sprinkled with the parsley and accompanied by new potatoes.

BEEF WITH GREEN PEAS

This is one of the most delightful and fragrant dishes of beef to be made with green peas.

Season a nice thick piece of beef steak and put it into a heavy pan, best enamelled, or a strong fireproof casserole with a good piece of butter. Cook for about ten minutes on a good heat, turning it frequently.

While this is going on, shell some small peas, the smallest you can get, and add them to the beef with a little more salt and pepper. They should fill up the sides between the meat and the pan and cover the top of the steak by about an inch.

Now put on the lid and simmer gently without further attention for two and a half to three hours. It is amazingly good, but do not cook more than you will eat hot, for it is disappointing when cold.

If you are using frozen peas add them 20 minutes before you want to serve the dish.

171

BEEFSTEAK TARTARE

This may well appeal to some as an unusual dish but raw meat is not to everyone's taste. We suggest you try this for yourself before serving it as a party piece. (It was originally made, round about the twelfth century, out of horse-flesh on which the Tartars subsisted.)

Chop up very finely, or put through a coarse mincer, some nice raw fillet of beef. Spread it out on a plate, sprinkle it with salt and pepper and mix it with some parsley and an egg-yolk.

Serve it cold on small rounds of toast which should not be too thick.

Note: There are always some who appreciate oddities, for various reasons. This, I think, is one of them. In Sweden they have the same thing, with anchovy fillet added.

Beefsteak Tartare

Crown roast of lamb

CROWN ROAST OF LAMB

This highly dramatic dish looks as if it ought to be British all right, but in fact it is of American origin.

Most butchers will be able to prepare the joint for you, as it is rather difficult to do this at home. It is in fact two best ends of neck of lamb containing a total of fourteen cutlets which still adhere to each other at their bases after the chine has been removed. It will come from the butcher's ready to cook, except for the filling and you must persuade him to mince the trimmings up for you. These can be mixed with sausage meat or simply with breadcrumbs and a seasoning of salt, pepper and mixed herbs. One of these mixtures properly moistened is then put into the middle of the crown, and the bones of the cutlets should be protected with a cube of bread or of fat bacon to prevent them from burning. A piece of greased paper or kitchen foil is placed over the stuffing, and the joint is roasted in a moderate oven for one and a half to two hours according to size.

Sometimes the crown is cooked unstuffed, in which case a suitably sized glass or earthenware bowl is put in the middle to keep the joint in shape.

When it is cooked the middle may be filled with mashed potatoes, boiled chestnuts put through a potato-ricer, Brussels sprouts, green peas or a whole cooked small cauliflower sprinkled with buttered crumbs. The joint is carved by separating the cutlets at the base. 173

MILANESE CUTLETS

Fried egg-and-breadcrumbed cutlets are sometimes rather dull, but not when they are done like this.

Trim the lamb cutlets nicely (not too much fat) and dip them in melted butter. Now cover them with a fifty-fifty mixture of fine breadcrumbs and grated Parmesan cheese. Shake off any loose crumbs and once more dip the cutlets into the butter and cover them again with the cheese and breadcrumb mixture. Dip them finally in the melted butter, and grill them gently and slowly.

Serve with a tomato sauce and spinach purée.

FRIED BREAST OF LAMB

Cook a piece of breast of lamb in a saucepan with a sprig of parsley, a bay leaf, a small onion stuck with half a dozen cloves, a teacupful of diced carrot and a quarter of a small turnip also diced. Add salt and a few peppercorns and cover the meat with boiling water. Skim when it boils again and cook gently until the bones will slip out.

Remove them and press the breast between two plates with a heavy plate on top. When quite cold, cut the meat into neat pieces, egg-and-breadcrumb these and fry them golden on each side in a little butter or lard.

Hand a tomato or thick brown sauce with them. Some people like pickled gherkins as an extra.

JUGGED LAMB

1 lb. well-trimmed lamb cutlets : 1 onion : $\frac{1}{2}$ oz. butter : 2 tomatoes : 1 dessertspoonful flour : $\frac{1}{2}$ pint stock : 1 lemon : salt, pepper and celery salt : 1 teaspoonful red currant jelly : chopped parsley : $\frac{1}{2}$ small glass of port wine.

Brown the quartered onion in the butter, transfer to a casserole and brown the cutlets on both sides in the same fat, putting them afterwards with the onions. Add two peeled medium tomatoes and a dessertspoonful of flour first browned in the fat from which the cutlets were taken.

Now stir smoothly in the stock seasoned with salt, pepper and celery salt, squeeze in the juice of a small lemon and cook, closely covered, in a moderately slow oven for two hours.

Ten minutes before serving stir in the red currant jelly, chopped parsley and port wine and finish cooking.

STUFFED MUTTON CHOPS

Take some loin chops and cut through the meat horizontally so that a deep pocket is made through to the bone.

Stuff this with any filling you like, forcemeat, sausage meat or sage and onion stuffing, and then press the sides of the chops lightly together again.

Now dip them in crumbs, then in beaten egg and then in crumbs again, and bake them in a hot oven until done, basting with butter or other suitable fat and turning them over once during the cooking, about a quarter of an hour on each side.

Serve garnished with sprigs of watercress.

VEAL CHOPS

Veal is inclined to be tasteless, and this treatment improves these chops.

4 veal chops : $\frac{1}{2}$ onion : 1 carrot : 2 sticks celery : 4 cloves : $\frac{1}{2}$ teaspoonful peppercorns : breadcrumbs : egg.

Put the chops in a saucepan with the carrot, onion and celery sliced and the spices in a muslin bag. Cover them with boiling water, skim and cook slowly until the meat is tender. Then drain the chops, and when they are cold, season them with salt and pepper, egg-and-breadcrumb them and fry golden on each side in butter.

Serve in a border of macaroni bound with onion sauce.

VEAL ESCALOPES WITH CREAM AND MUSTARD

Beat the veal cutlets as thin as possible and season them lightly with salt and pepper. Melt a little butter in a frying-pan and fry the escalopes until lightly browned on each side. Take them out and keep them hot. Now pour a little cream, say five or six tablespoonfuls, into the pan, and

Veal escalope

mix in a teaspoonful of French mustard. Stir and scrape over a moderate heat until the cream thickens a little and assumes a lovely café-au-lait colour. Pour this quickly over the escalopes, and serve with your best potato purée and some delicately flavoured vegetable, green peas for instance or even a creamy dish of spinach.

KNUCKLE OF VEAL

The Italians treat this part of the calf far better than the British. They call it Osso Buco. (Note for those who do not like it, the glass of wine may be omitted, but it will not be so good.)

3 lb. knuckle of veal sawn in two inch lengths : 1 onion : 1 carrot : 1 or 2 sticks celery : 1 oz. butter : 1 oz. flour : $\frac{1}{2}$ pint tomato pulp or diluted tomato purée : 1 glass dry white wine : bunch of parsley, thyme and bay leaf : lemon.

Brown the vegetables, chopped, in a little butter in a large saucepan, add the veal and brown this too. Add an ounce of butter kneaded with an ounce of flour, and brown this too. Now add the tomato pulp or purée, the wine and just enough water barely to cover the meat. Add the bunch of herbs, bring to the boil, cover and simmer gently for about an hour and a half. Strain the sauce on serving and add to it at the last moment a little strip of lemon peel chopped up very finely with a few sprigs of parsley.

Plain boiled rice should accompany it or if preferred, a white risotto (page 194).

176

POT PIE

This is real old English fare.

1 lb. raw lean veal : 4 oz. thin rashers of streaky green bacon : $\frac{1}{2}$ lb. half-boiled potatoes : short-crust pastry (see page 84).

Cut the veal into neat pieces and put them in a pie-dish in layers with the bacon slices, seasoning each with plenty of salt and pepper. Now three-quarters fill the dish with a well-flavoured stock made from the trimmings and any bones from the veal, and put another pie-dish of the same size upside down on top. Bake in a moderate oven for an hour and a half.

Now add more cold stock to replace what has reduced during the cooking and cover the top with the thickly sliced potatoes. Cover all with a pastry lid and bake again in a moderately hot oven for about three-quarters of an hour.

COLD SWEETBREAD FLAN

This dish, known in professional cookery as Ris de Veau à la Suédoise, is as pleasant a presentation of cold calf's sweetbreads as you can find.

Blanch and poach the sweetbreads without colouring them, and when they are quite cold, cut them into thin slices all the same size. Cut also some thin slices of cooked tongue the same shape and size. Spread each slice of sweetbread lightly with horseradish butter (creamed butter mixed with grated horseradish to taste) and cover with a piece of tongue.

Arrange these overlapping in a pastry flan case first cooked blind and then lined with a cooked vegetable salad bound with mayonnaise sauce, and place in the middle a small lettuce heart with the leaves opened out slightly. More mayonnaise may be handed separately, but there should be enough in the salad. Serve slightly chilled.

PORK WITH PRUNES

We have been getting used to eating fruit with meat from American cookery, this Swedish dish is both pleasant to eat and picturesque.

3½ lb. loin of pork : 20 stoned prunes : salt, white pepper and a small pinch of ground ginger : 1 pint white meat stock or even water.

Have the meat boned and prepared for rolling and stuff it down the middle with the prunes side by side, having first rinsed them in cold water and halved them. Rub the meat well with the seasonings, roll it up and tie it, and brown it quickly all over. Transfer it to a casserole or saucepan, pour the hot stock or water over it, put on the lid and simmer over a very low heat for about an hour and a half until tender. Serve with fried potato balls, apple sauce and more stewed prunes if you wish.

BAKED GAMMON OF BACON AND HAM

The Americanisation of some of our British food has been slowly taking place since the war, and nowhere is its influence felt more than in the realm of ham and bacon. The baked dishes of these joints are good to look at and intriguing to taste : they make party dishes which, being served cold, have the maximum of hostess appeal.

The gammon, or ham, is placed, fat side up-wards, in a baking-tin and baked in a low oven, allowing twenty-five minutes to the pound for a ten pound piece. Three-quarters of an hour before this time is reached, it is taken from the oven, the rind stripped off and it can then be treated in the following alternative ways.

(1) Go on basting it in a moderate oven with cider, pineapple juice, mixed fruit juices or thin honey or with the juice of an orange and a lemon and a breakfastcupful of sugar cooked together for five minutes.

(2) Trim the fat to an even half-inch thick-ness, and make criss-cross cuts about a quarter of an inch thick, sticking cloves in the diamonds if you wish. Then spread the whole surface with one of the following mixtures and put the meat back into a moderately hot oven for about a quarter of an hour for the coating to glaze evenly.

Spreadings:

(1) A breakfastcupful of brown sugar mois-tened with some of the drippings.

(2) A breakfastcupful of brown sugar mixed with three level dessertspoonfuls of flour or half a teacupful of fine breadcrumbs.

177

(3) A breakfastcupful of brown sugar moistened with three dessertspoonfuls of vinegar, cider or fruit juice.

(4) A breakfastcupful of brown sugar mixed with a level teaspoonful of mustard and three teaspoonfuls or so of vinegar, enough to make a spreadable paste.

An alternative way is first to boil the gammon or ham in the usual way and when it has cooled in the liquid to place it, fat side upwards in a baking-tin and bake in a moderate oven for half an hour. The skin is then stripped off, and the joint is treated as described above.

BARBECUED GAMMON RASHER

A typical example of the American treatment of ham or bacon.

Grill a good slice of gammon of bacon, letting the fat drop into the grilling-pan, and when it is done, transfer it to the serving-dish and add to the fat in the pan three tablespoonfuls of good vinegar, a tablespoonful and a half of made mustard, half a teaspoonful of caster sugar, a little paprika pepper and a tablespoonful of red currant jelly.

Heat well through, stirring, and pour over the gammon rasher to serve.

GAMMON RASHER WITH CREAM

During the first world war many dishes with gammon or ham were imported from Canada and are now becoming favourites again. This one, for example, somewhat glorifies the humble gammon rasher.

Gammon rasher of bacon, $\frac{1}{2}$ inch thick : butter : brown sugar : about $\frac{1}{2}$ pint thin cream.

Soak the rasher if necessary (if it is too salty), rinse it and wipe it quite dry. Now fry it in very little butter until a light brown, sprinkling it with a little brown sugar if you like. It should take about twenty minutes altogether, ten minutes on each side, and must be turned frequently. When it is done transfer it to the serving-dish and pour the cream into the pan in which it was cooked. Bring to the boil and stirring all the time let it thicken a little, when it should be poured over the rasher and sprinkled with chopped parsley.

BACON AND KIDNEYS

Get as many sheep's kidneys as you want, skin them, remove the white gristly centre and season with salt and pepper. Roll each half in a thin rasher of streaky bacon, transfix with a cocktail stick or tie round with cotton and bake in a moderate oven until the bacon is crisp.

A more substantial way is to make a simple forcemeat (Volume One, page 66) with chopped parsley, onion, breadcrumbs and egg, and spread this on the bacon rashers first. Then place the prepared kidney or kidney half on this, roll it up and tie it and bake in a hot oven for twenty minutes or so. Serve on buttered toasts.

BACON, ONION AND APPLE PIE

Short crust pastry made with $\frac{1}{2}$ lb. flour, (see page 84) : $\frac{1}{2}$ lb. bacon rashers : 1 lb. onions : 1 lb. cooking apples : 1 tablespoonful caster sugar : 2 teaspoonfuls dried sage : salt and pepper.

Cut the rind from the bacon and line a pie-dish with the rashers. Put the sliced onions on this bed and sprinkle them with salt, pepper and half the dried sage. Cover this with the sliced peeled and cored apples and sprinkle these with more salt and pepper, the rest of the sage and the caster sugar. Add a teacupful of water and cover with the pastry.

Bake in a moderate oven for an hour and a quarter.

YORKSHIRE BACON CUSTARD

6 thin rashers of streaky smoked bacon : 2 eggs : short crust pastry.

Line a pie-plate with the pastry, cut the bacon into narrow strips and cover the bottom with it.

Beat the eggs well and season them with salt and pepper, pour them over the bacon, cover with a thin pastry top and bake in a moderate oven for about half an hour. Eat hot or cold.

KEBAB

If the eighteenth or nineteenth centuries popularised Curry in this country, the Near East did the same for cooking on skewers in the twentieth. These savoury morsels, of which there are very many variations, have come to be known under the general name of Kebab, and usually take the form of alternate pieces of meat, usually mutton or lamb, onion, bay leaf, tomato, bacon and mushrooms. The simplest kind however, are the best, and the secret of success lies in rapid cooking and preliminary soaking in a marinade. Here is a typical example :

For six people. 2 lb. of leg of mutton or lamb : 1 large onion : 1 tablespoonful olive oil.

Cut the meat from the bone, remove skin and fat and cut into one-inch cubes. Extract the juice from the onion, mix it with the olive oil in a bowl and put the pieces of mutton into this marinade. Leave them for not less than an hour, turning them over now and then. Allowing six pieces to each skewer, stick them on about half an inch apart, and grill them rapidly and fiercely, turning the skewers all the time. The best authorities say that although green peppers, tomatoes, mushrooms or onion rings can be served as a garnish, it is advisable to grill these separately, as their presence on the skewers with the meat tends to toughen it.

An interesting Greek version (where this skewer dish is known as souvlakia), gives veal or pork as alternatives to the lamb and marinates the pieces for half an hour in a mixture of two tablespoonfuls of olive oil, the juice of half a lemon, salt, pepper and a level teaspoonful of dried oregano or wild marjoram. They are then threaded on the skewers with bits of bay leaf between each pair.

Kebabs

The savoury skewerfuls are generally served on a bed of pilaff rice, which is made as follows:

Pilaff rice

8 oz. Patna Rice: $\frac{1}{2}$ teaspoonful salt: 1 oz. butter: $\frac{3}{4}$ pint well-flavoured white meat stock.

Wash and dry the rice, and melt the butter in a large saucepan. Pour in the stock, season with the salt and bring to the boil fairly quickly. Now pour in the rice and cook at the same temperature for five minutes with the lid on. Then turn the heat very low and cook for seven or eight minutes, when the stock should all be absorbed, and the rice cooked. Now take the pan from the heat, put a cloth over the top with the lid on top of it and leave on the lowest possible heat for half an hour. This part of the process is most important, as the cloth dries up the steam from the rice and results in the grains being separate. Last of all, stir gently with a fork, and add another ounce or so of melted butter. The flavour of the rice depends of course on the flavour of the stock, which should be rich and oniony.

SAUSAGES WITH CABBAGE

This is a dish which ought to be thoroughly English, if the French had not beaten us to it!

Cut a cabbage into fairly small pieces and cook these until half done in salted water with a few bacon bones or, better still, in the water in which a piece of pickled pork was boiled. By the time the cabbage is ready, have some sausages grilled and then put half the cabbage, well-drained, chopped up and mixed with a little of the fat from the grilling of the sausages, into a deep fireproof dish, seasoning well with pepper and grated nutmeg, or better still if you can get them, a few crushed dried juniper berries.

Lay the sausages on top, cover them with the rest of the cabbage, pour over half a pint of beef stock or the like, and bake for half an hour or so in a moderate oven.

SAUSAGES WITH CARROTS

Quite a grand dish with far from grand ingredients which owes its special taste to the glass of dry white wine which is essential.

Stew some baby carrots whole in butter and then cut them in slices. Put them into a shallow fireproof dish in which they will be served, and arrange on them some grilled chipolata sausages.

Sprinkle these with a little chopped parsley, some chopped fried onions, some of the fat from the grilling of the sausages, a drop or two of lemon juice and a glass of dry white wine. Cook all together in a moderate oven for about ten minutes, and serve as it is, with mashed potato.

SAUSAGES IN BEER

This should appeal to the beer drinkers of today.

1 lb. sausages : salt, bay leaf and peppercorns : $\frac{3}{4}$ pint draught beer, old or mild : brown roux : mixed spice.

Put the sausages into a bowl, pour boiling water over them, leave them for a minute, then dry them and brown them all over in a little fat to which you have added a little salt and the bay leaf and half a dozen peppercorns. Add $\frac{1}{2}$ pint of the beer, bring quickly to the boil and boil for a few minutes to reduce it a little. Now add some more beer, enough to replace what has boiled away and to cover the sausages. Let them simmer for a quarter of an hour.

Strain off and thicken the sauce with the roux, adding a pinch of mixed spice, and pour this over the sausages which you have bedded in a comfortable border of mashed potato.

MEAT HEDGEHOG

This is a meaty version of the very striking sweet hedgehog trifle, which will be found on page 227.

$1\frac{1}{2}$ lb. minced cooked or raw meat, well seasoned and including some bacon or ham if possible : 6 oz. mashed potato : 6 oz. breadcrumbs : 1 egg : fat bacon.

Mix all the ingredients well together and bind with a beaten egg. Mould it into your idea of what a hedgehog is shaped like, and insert all over it and pretty closely together some strips of fat bacon about a quarter inch by a quarter inch and two to three inches long. These should protrude about an inch and when cooked represent the animal's spines. Roast it in the usual way without basting it (as this tends to make it fall apart) for three-quarters of an hour or so, more if the meat is raw.

Cook it in the dish in which it will be served, surrounded by a nice mixture of vegetables and accompanied by a boat of thick gravy.

KIDNEYS WITH SHERRY

Skin and cut some sheep's kidneys into thin slices and brown them very quickly in a little butter in a frying-pan. Now add a pinch of flour, mix it in well and season with salt and pepper.

Moisten with a little stock and a tablespoonful or two of sherry and cook all together for a few minutes only, for over-cooked kidneys are always tough. Cream can be added to your taste.

KIDNEYS ON SKEWERS

Cut the skinned sheep's kidneys in halves or thickish slices and impale these on skewers, one for each person, alternating them with a slice of bacon cut to size and a slice of mushroom. Dip each skewerful in melted butter and then in breadcrumbs and again in butter. Cook them under a medium grill. Serve with sauté potatoes and sprigs of watercress.

KIDNEY DUMPLING

This and the next recipe are particularly interest-

ing country ways of making a meal out of a kidney.

For each person 1 large onion : 1 sheep's kidney : suet crust.

Cut a large onion in halves crosswise and scoop out as much of the middle as will leave a cavity large enough to hold a skinned sheep's kidney cut in quarters. Season with salt and pepper and put the two halves together again.

Wrap the whole thing up in suet crust (Volume One, page 90), and bake in a moderate oven for about an hour. It must on no account be boiled.

KIDNEY POTATO

For each person cut a large potato in halves and scoop out a cavity in each half in exactly the same way as directed above. Put in the seasoned kidney, tie the two halves together again tightly with string (to prevent as much kidney gravy as possible from escaping) and bake very slowly in a moderate oven until the potato is tender.

GRILLED PIG'S TROTTERS

A way with a plebeian dish which will be found excellent indeed.

Get the butcher to cut the prepared trotters in halves lengthways and wrap up each half in a piece of cloth or butter muslin, twisting and tying each end of the little parcel well.

Now cook them for four or five hours in salted water with peppercorns, whole allspice, a large

Sauté kidneys in sherry

bunch of parsley, thyme and bay leaf and one or two cloves of garlic.

When they are done, take them out of the water, let them get cold and unwrap them. Roll them in olive oil and then in breadcrumbs, and grill them quickly. A quarter of an hour should be enough.

CASSEROLE OF TRIPE

One of the famous dishes of the world, Tripe à la mode de Caen ennobles this homely fare to the highest degree.

2 lb. fine double tripe : 1 ox foot : 1 calf's foot : 2 or 3 pieces of the rind of fresh or pickled pork, 2 carrots : 4 onions : a bunch of parsley, thyme, bay leaf and celery : 1 clove garlic : 4 spice cloves : salt : pinch of cayenne pepper : 1 liqueurglassful brandy or, better, apple brandy (Calvados) : dry cider.

Blanch the tripe for half an hour ; drain and dry it and cut it into small squares, as well as the meat of the ox and calf's foot. Put in the bottom of a large casserole the pieces of pork rind, the bones from the two feet, the carrots and onions cut in small pieces, the bunch of herbs, the 183 seasonings and pieces of tripe and meat. Pour over them the brandy and enough dry cider to cover the contents of the casserole. Put on the lid and seal as hermetically as possible with a flour-and-water paste round the cover. Bring just to the boil and cook in a slow oven for eight hours. On serving remove the bones, vegetables and bunch of herbs and take off as much grease as possible from the gravy. It should be served, and kept, as hot as possible.

OX TAIL

1 ox tail : 1 carrot : 1 onion : 1 stick of celery : 1 small turnip : 1 oz. flour : 1 oz. dripping or lard : 1 quart good meat stock or diluted meat cubes : a sprig of parsley, thyme and a bay leaf in a muslin bag with peppercorns, and a blade of mace.

The butcher will have cut the tail in pieces for you. Blanch these by bringing them to the boil in cold water and boiling for five minutes. Then drain well and wipe dry, coat them with seasoned flour and fry them in the fat until golden.

Transfer them to a casserole or saucepan with the vegetables cut in pieces. Add the herbs and spices and just cover them with the stock. Bring just to the boil, cover the pan closely and stew gently until the meat is tender, which will take from four to five hours according to the age of the tail.

Make a brown roux with the ounce of fat and flour and add enough of the cooking liquor to make a nice thick brown gravy, in the cooking of which you can add a glass of claret or other suitable light red wine. Pour this over the pieces of tail and garnish with pieces of the vegetables.

LAMB AND PEAS

A Victorian dish rejoicing in the extraordinary name of China Cholla, which sounds in the best tradition of the British Empire.

My reference says simply : A luncheon dish.

2 lb. best end of neck of lamb : 1 pint shelled green peas : 2 oz. butter : 2 good-sized lettuces : a little stock.

Cut the lamb into small squares and shred the lettuces. Put them with the peas, butter and stock into a saucepan and cook with the lid tightly on for a couple of hours.

The thickened cooking liquid will make the appropriate sauce.

Poultry and Game

FRIED CHICKEN

Everywhere one goes nowadays it is always fried chicken that confronts one, the little joints usually coated with egg-and-breadcrumbs, fried in deep fat or oil and accompanied by fried sweet corn cakes and fried bananas, masquerading under the name of Chicken Maryland.

This chicken dish is another of our fairly recent importations from America and it might be as well to be authentic about it, for the American dish is quite different from the British travesties of it.

The little chickens known as broilers today are generally used, served in halves to supply two persons, but larger birds weighing about two and a half pounds can be cut in pieces and will serve four to six.

Dip the halves or pieces in cold milk or water and drain but do not wipe them. Sprinkle them with salt and pepper and coat them as thickly as possible with flour. Cook them in a heavy frying-pan, putting them into a little shallow very hot but not smoking fat and browning them quickly all over. Then add half a teacupful of boiling water, cover and either reduce the heat or put the pan into a moderate oven. It will take from thirty-five to sixty minutes to cook them, according to the size of the birds.

They are then put on to a hot dish and kept hot while you make one of the following gravies, which is poured over them on serving:

Make a sauce with an ounce and a half of fat in the pan and an ounce of flour and one of the following moistenings:

(1) $\frac{3}{4}$ pint chicken stock or diluted bouillon cube.
(2) $\frac{1}{2}$ pint stock and $\frac{1}{4}$ pint cream.
(3) Cream alone, being careful to scrape and stir in the drippings in the pan.

Choice can be made among the fats in which the chicken is fried:

(1) 3 oz. butter.
(2) 1 oz. butter and 2 oz. lard.
(3) 2 oz. olive oil or cooking oil.
(4) 3 oz. smoked or green bacon dripping.

Serve the dish garnished as you will.

CHAUDFROID OF CHICKEN

An example of decoration referred to on page 160 (Salmon in Aspic), but of a simpler kind.

1 cold boiled fowl: 1 pint white sauce made with milk and the stock from boiling the fowl: 1 oz. powdered gelatine: $\frac{1}{2}$ pint aspic jelly: truffle or black olives: sweet peppers: mushroom: olives: lemon rind: green part of a leek.

Cut the chicken into neat joints, trim them and chill them in the refrigerator. Warm the sauce and add the gelatine dissolved in a little hot water, passing the whole through a muslin cloth, for it is important to get it as glossily smooth as possible. When cool enough coat the chicken joints with it, decorate them with whatever you fancy, let it set and then cover each

Chaudfroid of chicken

with the half-melted aspic jelly with a table-spoon.

If preferred the whole chicken can be decorated and coated in this way, as in the photograph. At home you may find it better to have the portions ready for each person rather than to carve the chicken at the table which destroys much of the beauty of its appearance.

CHICKEN EN COCOTTE BONNE FEMME

The French have many attractive ways of dealing with chicken, and this one is particularly convenient for dealing with small birds or the joints of chicken so popular today.

4 quarter-chickens : 2–3 rashers streaky green bacon : $\frac{1}{2}$ oz. butter : $\frac{3}{4}$ lb. potatoes : button onions.

Cut the bacon into small dice and fry them in the butter until some of their fat exudes. Take them out and in the same fat fry the pieces of chicken all over until golden, take these out too and in the same fat fry the potatoes cut in not too thin rounds, the button onions and the mushrooms. If you like a specially hammy flavour add at the same time some small cubes of cooked ham. Now put all the ingredients

186

into the casserole with the fat from their frying, but no added liquid. Sprinkle with salt and pepper and put on the lid as tightly as you can. Bake in a moderate oven for about an hour until the chicken is tender, and serve as it is, though at the very end there could be added a little clear veal gravy or strong diluted meat bouillon, though this is not essential.

Chicken en cocotte bonne femme

CHICKEN WITH RED WINE

Those who like cooking with wine should try this dish of Coq au Vin on the next party occasion. The French recipe demands the use of the chicken's blood as a thickening agent, but as this is usually impossible in this country, I have adopted an easier way which will be found good enough by most.

Cut the chicken into pieces, sprinkle them with salt, pepper and mixed spice and leave them for two or three hours. An hour and a half before you want to eat, fry in butter some small cubes of breast of pickled pork or green bacon and a dozen small onions, using a pan large enough to hold the pieces of bird. When the onions are golden, add the chicken joints and fry these golden, too. Pour away the butter, add a liqueurglassful of brandy to the chicken and set it alight. When the flames have died down, enrich with a bottle of red Burgundy or a red wine approximating to this and season with salt, freshly-ground black pepper, a pinch of sugar, a crushed clove of garlic, and a bunch of parsley, thyme and bay leaf. Simmer gently, covered, for an hour, then take the pieces of chicken out and thicken the sauce in the usual way with butter and flour. Pour this over the chicken and garnish with triangular croutons of fried bread.

CHICKEN WITH SAFFRON RICE

Braise the chicken (see Braising, Volume One, page 46) with a glass of white wine and the same of stock, a large onion stuck with three cloves, a few small onions, two or three quartered tomatoes, a clove of garlic (if you like) and a bunch of parsley, thyme, bay leaf, celery and tarragon. When cooked, keep it warm and strain off the braising liquor.

Cook a tablespoonful of finely chopped onion lightly without colouring in half an ounce of lard or butter. Add to this a breakfastcupful of drained Carolina rice and let this cook for a minute or two, stirring, until it becomes quite opaque. Now take the braising liquor and add to it enough good white stock to make up two and a half breakfastcupfuls of it in all, and pour this over the rice. Season with salt and pepper, a good pinch of saffron and a suspicion of nutmeg. After bringing to the boil cook in a moderate oven with the lid on for about half an hour when the liquid should be all absorbed and the rice cooked and gloriously golden. Put the chicken on a dish, and serve with the saffron rice round it.

GIBLET PIE

An excellent way of illustrating the precept waste not, want not, but an admirable old dish in its own right.

2 or 3 sets of chicken giblets : 2 onions : 2 carrots : chicken stock or water : $\frac{3}{4}$ lb. beef steak : 6 oz. pastry.

Put the giblets into a saucepan with the onions and carrots cut in dice, just cover them with stock or water and let them simmer gently for an hour. Then drain the giblets and cut into neat pieces. Cut the beef steak into similar sized pieces, roll each in flour seasoned with salt and pepper and put a layer of these in the bottom of your pie dish. Cover these with the drained vegetables and then put the giblets upon them. Finish with the rest of the beef, season with salt and pepper and pour in enough of the giblet cooking liquor to come half-way up the dish.

Cover with a pastry crust to your liking and bake in a moderately hot oven for three-quarters of an hour to an hour. Serve hot.

KROMESKIS OF CHICKEN

In many households there is often an embarrassingly small amount of cold chicken left to the next day, but here is a good way of making it go as far as possible, and deliciously too. These fritters can, of course, be made with any sort of cold meat, but chicken seems to me to be the best.

Make a thick white sauce (panada, page 25) to bind the minced cold chicken and thicken it with an egg-yolk, if you like. When this is cold, shape it with floured hands into pieces like large corks, and roll these up in thin pieces of cooked ham or bacon cut to a suitable size. Coat these in turn with fritter batter (Volume One, page 106) and fry them in deep fat or oil.

Serve garnished with spinach or French beans or both, and hand a tomato sauce with them.

WILD DUCK AND ORANGE SALAD

Roast the duck as directed in Volume One, page 63, and serve with an orange salad prepared like this.

Orange salad

4 oranges : chopped parsley : oil and vinegar dressing.

Cut the skin off the oranges in such a way as to remove the pith and leaving only the actual flesh of the fruit exposed. Then cut down between the segments towards the centre so that you have only segments of the flesh left. Take out any pips left behind and squeeze out the juice from the pithy remains.

Arrange the sections on a bed of lettuce or watercress and pour over them a French oil-and-vinegar dressing (a dessertspoonful of vinegar to two of olive oil with salt and pepper) to which you have added a little of the orange juice. If you do not like vinegar, as some do not, use all orange juice in its place. Finally sprinkle with a little chopped parsley on top of the orange.

WOOD PIGEONS WITH BEER

On the Continent they cook these birds in wine, but we do so in beer like this.

When the wood pigeons are cleaned, keep back the livers and blanch them, as they will be used in the stuffing which is an ordinary savoury one (Volume One, page 66) to which the 189 chopped livers are added. Season this rather highly with salt, pepper and nutmeg and stuff the birds with it.

Now put them into a saucepan with a tight-fitting lid, adding a pint of water, a glass of draught mild ale, a roughly chopped onion and a few sprigs of parsley and a bay leaf.

Let the pigeons stew gently until they are tender, the length of time depending on their age, but it will not be much less than two hours,

then strain off the liquid and thicken it with browned flour and butter. Serve the pigeons with this sauce strained over them and garnished with triangular sippets of toast or fried bread.

PARTRIDGES EN CASSEROLE

Old birds are used for this, easier to obtain and much cheaper.

Cook gently in the casserole with a small

Wood pigeons with beer

piece of butter for about half an hour some small dice of bacon (or a bacon bone or two) and sliced onion and carrot. Take the casserole off the heat, season with salt and pepper and add a tablespoonful or two, no more, of well-flavoured stock.

Meanwhile you will have stuffed the birds with sausage meat, and tied down over the breast of each a nice piece of fat bacon. Lay them on the bed of vegetables, put on the lid and cook very gently until they are tender which will take anything from an hour to two hours according to their age. When they are done, add a few spring or button onions first lightly fried all over, put the lid on again and cook on until the onions are tender too. The gravy should not be thickened, but just poured, after straining, over each partridge.

A few lightly fried button mushrooms could be added at the same time as the onions, if liked.

SADDLE OF HARE WITH CREAM

Get the butcher to prepare you the saddle of a young hare, by removing the two skins on the back right down to the flesh and cutting short the ribs so that the joint will stand up in the roasting dish. Put some thin rashers of green fattish bacon over the top, and bake it in a moderate oven on a bed of chopped carrots and onions and a sprig of rosemary for half an hour to forty minutes according to the age of the hare.

When it is nearly done, take off the bacon and remove the vegetables and rosemary with a perforated spoon, drain off the fat and pour into the pan a teacupful of cream. Stir this well with the juices left in the pan, and let it boil up to thicken. Finish with a few drops of lemon juice, and pour over the hare to serve. (The meat is carved in long thin strips down the length of the back.)

GAME PIE

Hot water crust pastry (Volume One, page 89) using 8 oz. flour: 1 pheasant: 1 lb. lean rump steak: 1 rasher of bacon: 3 sliced hard-boiled eggs: a little stock: salt and pepper to taste: a pinch of ground mace.

Well grease a raised pie-mould and line it with the pastry, reserving enough to make a lid You can get specially hinged moulds for game pies.

Cut the steak into cubes, divide the pheasant into neat joints or, if you feel inclined and have enough patience, bone it carefully and cut into cubes. Dice the bacon.

Fill the pie with the pheasant, steak, bacon and sliced egg on top, and season. Add a little stock and cover with a lid of pastry. Make a hole in the centre and decorate with a few pastry leaves made from the trimmed scraps. Bake in a hot oven, 450° F or Regulo 8 for half an hour then reduce to 375° F or Regulo 5 for one hour. Remove the mould and cook for a further half an hour. Fill with a little hot stock and allow to cool.

191

Curry

I suppose that curry was introduced into this country from India in the 18th or 19th centuries, but by Victorian times it had become as firmly entrenched as an almost national dish, as acclimatised as macaroni cheese. There are almost as many ways of making a curry as there are cooks who favour this very savoury form of food, and the one that follows exemplifies the general pattern.

The two principal ingredients beside the meat you are currying are well-flavoured stock and some coconut milk (the making of which is described below) and, of course, a first class proprietary curry powder and paste, though there are experts who prefer to make their own.

MEAT CURRY

The coconut milk demanded here is not the milk from inside the nut, but an infusion made in this way. Put some grated fresh coconut or desiccated coconut into a saucepan with enough cold water just to cover it, bring to the boil and then let it stand, off the heat, for twenty minutes. Press through a strainer and the result is what you want. Measure out a breakfastcupful and keep it by. Measure out also a breakfastcupful of the stock.

Now put two ounces of butter into a saucepan and in it fry to a light gold two small onions and a small clove of garlic very finely minced. Stir in a heaped tablespoonful of the curry powder and the same of the paste and cook it with the lid on over a low heat for three or four minutes. Then add by degrees a teacupful of the coconut milk and all of the stock, simmer for about a quarter of an hour and keep hot.

Now flour the pieces of raw meat, and fry them in another pan in an ounce of butter with a small onion cut in pieces. Turn them over with two wooden spoons (to avoid pricking them) until they are lightly browned all over, then take them out and put them into the hot curry mixture in the first pan. Leave them there for at least half an hour, adding a little more stock if they are not quite covered. Add now also a bay leaf and a teaspoonful of lemon juice, and cook, covered, on the lowest possible heat until the meat is tender. Then add another teacupful of coconut milk, and cook on for another five minutes or so.

If the sauce is not thick enough by then, you can reduce it by taking the lid off the pan and cooking it further. Use no flour for thickening, as the meat has already been floured sufficiently. When the curry is ready, you can correct the seasoning with a little salt and it is an improvement if a very little syrup from mango chutney is stirred in.

Curries made from fresh meat are the best, but you can use this sauce in making them from cooked or even tinned meat. Many contend that curries taste better when made the day before and warmed up, and there is some truth in this. But if you wish to keep them in this way see that they are kept in a bowl or pudding basin,

as they are unpleasant if kept in a metal sauce-pan or container.

FISH CURRY

A very simple curry sauce that I have come across seems to me particularly well-suited to use with cooked fish or indeed eggs. This is how it is made.

Fry a couple of small onions and, if you take my advice, half a small clove of garlic, all finely sliced, in two ounces of butter. When a light golden colour, stir in a tablespoonful of curry powder (or powder and paste half and half), and season with a little salt.

Now add half a pound of peeled and quartered tomatoes and a very little water, enough to make a thickish sauce, simmer very gently for about twenty minutes and then put in the large flakes of cooked fish, or some shellfish such as prawns, shrimps or lobster and cook on very gently indeed for another quarter of an hour.

The flavour of tomatoes goes exceptionally well with curry and is far better as a slight sweetener than the apples which some cooks use in making their version.

193

All curries are served with plainly boiled and well drained Patna rice, and other accompaniments such as desiccated coconut, Bombay Duck, Poppadums, various chutneys, etc., each served on a separate little dish, and taken at the whim of the eater.

Risotto

The famous dish of rice, the Italian risotto, is much the same in its ingredients as the Pilaff (page 180), but cooked in a different way. In its simplest form it is exemplified by the White Risotto, but a more popular form in this country today is the Risotto Milanese; recipes for both are given below.

WHITE RISOTTO

To every $\frac{1}{2}$ lb. of Carolina or Italian rice : $\frac{3}{4}$ pint well-flavoured white stock : $\frac{1}{2}$ small onion : $1\frac{3}{4}$ oz. butter : $\frac{3}{4}$ oz. grated Parmesan cheese.

Lightly brown the chopped onion in half the butter in a saucepan, add the rice and mix well together. Then add the boiling stock and mix well together and boil for about a quarter of an hour until the rice is cooked and the stock absorbed. Season with salt and pepper, and off the fire stir in the rest of the butter and the grated cheese.

RISOTTO MILANESE

For $\frac{1}{2}$ lb. Carolina or Italian rice : $\frac{1}{2}$ small onion : 2 oz. butter : 3 dessertspoonfuls dry white wine : $\frac{3}{4}$ pint chicken stock : $\frac{1}{4}$ teaspoonful saffron powder : salt, pepper and 2 oz. grated cheese.

Cook the chopped onions in half the butter until they are a light gold colour, then add the rice and cook on a moderate heat for a quarter of an hour, stirring all the time with a wooden spoon. Now add gradually the saffron powder, the wine and the boiling stock by degrees, mix all well together and season with salt and pepper. Simmer still stirring, for about half an hour, then add the cheese and the rest of the butter. A richer risotto will be obtained if you add an ounce of chopped raw beef marrow at the start.

Pasta

(INCLUDING MACARONI AND SPAGHETTI)

There are a large number of pasta of varying shapes and sizes, and although the simpler kind can easily be made at home, in this country they are usually bought dried. Instructions for cooking them are generally to be found on the packet, but two points must be always remembered. One is to cook them in plenty of boiling salted water, and the other is to see that they do not cook until they are flabby, but have a 'bite' in them. Fifteen to twenty minutes' boiling is about right if the pasta has not been in the grocer's for too long, and when done it should be drained and turned into the hot dish ready to receive it. A little hot olive oil can first be poured into the dish or a good piece of butter left to melt on top after it has been put into the dish.

I find that it is a good idea to turn the cooked pasta into a sieve immediately after cooking and to run the hot tap over it and let it drain before turning it into the dish.

There are a good number of sauces used to serve with the pasta in Italy, and these can either be mixed with it or served separately in a sauce boat. As an example, a recipe of the best-known in this country, Ragu Bolognese, is given here.

BOLOGNESE SAUCE

The proliferation of Espresso coffee bars seems to have had an immediate effect on our native eating habits, and there must be very few who do not recognise the words Spaghetti Bolog- nese. This is the sauce used in all Italian pasta dishes bearing its name.

To make enough to go with six good helpings of the chosen pasta: ½ lb. minced lean beef: ¼ lb. chickens' livers: 3 oz. streaky bacon, preferably green: 1 carrot: 1 onion: 1 small stick celery: 3 teaspoonfuls tinned tomato purée: 1 wineglassful of dry white wine: twice as much stock or water: ½ oz. butter: salt, pepper and nutmeg.

Cut the bacon into small dice and brown them slowly in a small saucepan in the butter. Now add the finely chopped onion, carrot, and celery and cook on until they are browned too. Add the beef and go on cooking, turning over with a fork, until this too is evenly browned. It is now time to add the chopped chickens' livers, then stir in the tomato purée and lastly the wine. Season to taste and finally moisten with the stock or water. Put on the lid and simmer gently for half to three-quarters of an hour. Mix well with the pasta before serving very hot, and at the very end stir in a piece of butter. Grated cheese should be handed separately.

MACARONI, SICILIAN FASHION

3 oz. macaroni: 4 oz. minced cooked chicken: 2 oz. minced cooked mushrooms: 1 dessert-spoonful minced parsley: salt and pepper: white or brown sauce.

Boil the macaroni for fifteen minutes and when it is cold cut it into short lengths and put a layer of these in a deep fireproof baking-dish which you have first well-buttered and then sprinkled all over with the parsley. On this put alternate layers of the mixed mince and macaroni, sprinkling each well with more grated cheese and seasoning with salt and pepper. When the dish is full, moisten with white or brown sauce (Volume One, page 22) according to your preference. Heat through thoroughly in the oven and at the last minute brown the top under the grill.

MACARONI TIMBALE

A decorative dish which is surprisingly simple to make, and a good substitute for Shepherd's pie when cold meat has to be dealt with.

$\frac{1}{2}$ lb. cooked meat : 2 oz. breadcrumbs : $\frac{1}{4}$ pint stock : 2 eggs : salt, pepper and nutmeg : $\frac{1}{4}$ lb. uncut macaroni.

Make your favourite and most savoury mixture of the minced meat, breadcrumbs, beaten eggs and stock and do not forget a touch of nutmeg in the seasoning.

While you are doing this boil the macaroni in salted water until tender, drain it and when cool enough to handle line a buttered pudding-basin with it, a circular curl over the bottom and upright strips on the sides. Put the meat mixture into this, carefully so as not to disturb the macaroni, then cover with buttered greaseproof paper or kitchen foil and steam for half to three-quarters of an hour until firm. Turn out and serve

with a tomato sauce poured round, not over it.

MACARONI CHEESE

3 oz. macaroni : 1 oz. butter : 1 oz. flour : a scant pint milk : 1 teaspoonful made mustard : 4 oz. grated cheese : breadcrumbs.

First cook and drain the macaroni, cut up in small pieces if you like. Make a white sauce with the butter, flour and milk and season with salt, pepper and mustard. Stir in the cheese keeping back a tablespoonful or two. When the cheese has melted, add the macaroni to the sauce and pour into a buttered dish. Sprinkle the top with the reserved grated cheese mixed with some breadcrumbs, and bake until the top is brown in a moderate oven.

SPAGHETTI WITH MUSHROOMS

$\frac{1}{2}$ lb. mushrooms : $\frac{1}{2}$ pint milk : 4 oz. spaghetti : 1 oz. butter : 2 oz. grated cheese, preferably Parmesan : butter.

Boil up the chopped stalks and peelings of the mushrooms, first well washed, in the milk until it is flavoured with them. Strain them off and thicken the milk with butter and flour and cook in this the mushroom caps cut in largish squares and seasoned with salt and pepper. Keep hot while you cook the spaghetti as shown on page 195, drain it and mix in the butter and cheese.

Line a buttered fireproof dish with the spaghetti, leaving a hollow in the middle, and into this pour the mushrooms and their cooking liquor. Cover the top with the rest of the spaghetti, smooth it flat and scatter over it more grated cheese and some thin flakes of butter.

Put the dish into the oven until the top is a nice golden-brown, and serve.

NOODLES

A thin ribbon-like form of pasta is known in Italy under the name of tagliatelle. This form has become popularised in Austria and Germany as nudeln, in France as nouilles and in England under the slightly ridiculous one of noodles. This is cooked in the same way as any other pasta, but there is one special fashion of serving them in Alsace, which appeals to the simpler palates.

Alsatian Noodles

$\frac{1}{2}$ lb. noodles : $2\frac{3}{4}$ pints water : salt : $2\frac{3}{4}$ oz. butter : bread.

Bring the water to the boil, add salt to taste and the noodles and cook them over a low heat for twenty minutes or so until tender but still firm. Bake a piece of bread (French loaf is more authentic) until it is golden brown and crush it coarsely with a rolling-pin. Meanwhile melt the butter.

Drain the noodles thoroughly, turn them into the serving dish, sprinkle them fairly thickly with the baked crumbs and just before serving, pour the melted butter over the top.

PIZZA

Here is another favourite introduced here by the Italian espresso coffee bars and rapidly becoming adopted by many. It makes a good substantial meal and can vary a good deal in the matter of its contents. The pizza napoletana is the most popular version.

For the dough: $\frac{1}{4}$ lb. plain flour : scant $\frac{1}{4}$ oz. yeast : tepid water : salt.

For the filling: 4 large ripe tomatoes : 6 anchovy fillets : 3 oz. Italian mozzarella cheese : chopped fresh or dried marjoram (oregano) : olive oil.

Make the dough as you would for bread (Volume One, page 118), and when ready roll it into a ball and leave it on a plate in a warm place, covered with a cloth for a good two hours, until it has doubled its volume. Then roll it out to a circle about a quarter of an inch thick, which will be about eight inches across.

Peel and chop the tomatoes roughly, spread them on top of the pizza, sprinkling with salt and pepper and put halves of the anchovy fillets here and there on top. Finally add the cheese (which can be bought in most delicatessen shops) cut in small thin slices. Sprinkle with plenty of marjoram and moisten with olive oil. Put into a round baking-tin a little larger in diameter, having first poured a little olive oil into it, so as to allow the pizza to expand. Bake in a hot oven for twenty to thirty minutes and to eat it at its best serve immediately it is done.

Vegetables

The British cook has never been renowned for her treatment of vegetables and this is easily understandable in a country where meat or fish and two veg. has been for so long the rule. But there are signs that education in the use of vegetables is beginning to bear fruit and we are now much more adaptable in this respect.

In the following pages will be found some old favourites of past years that may have now been forgotten as well as some recipes from overseas to add to our variety. Among these I would like to note the Jerusalem artichoke chips as a change from the omnipresent potato crisp; the fried cauliflowers and tiny Brussels sprouts (for which the frozen kind are so useful); the hot red cabbage; fried parsley which makes such a usefully different garnish; the way to cook green peas in the French way and the deliciously buttery baked potato mould, pommes Anna. I should also like to recommend to those who find their home-grown produce catches up too fast on them the ways suggested for dealing with this problem, by getting away from the idea that vegetables cannot form a dish in their own right.

ASPARAGUS FRITTERS

Get some thinnish asparagus and boil it just a trifle underdone. Cut off the edible tips and when they are quite cold, tie a few together in little bundles (three or four heads are enough) and dip them in your best coating batter. Then fry these in deep fat or oil, remembering to remove the tying cotton before serving.

This is a good way of using the very thin heads, called sprue, which are difficult to eat in the accepted way.

FRENCH OR RUNNER BEANS WITH CHEESE

The simplest way of making this pleasant dish is to cook the beans in the ordinary way, and after draining them well to serve them coated with a cheese sauce (Volume One, page 22) in the making of which you have used a little of the liquid the beans were cooked in instead of some of the usual milk.

The second way is to put the drained cooked beans in a shallow buttered fireproof dish. Season them with salt, pepper and a touch of cayenne, then add a teacupful of grated cheese, a level tablespoonful of melted butter and half a teacupful of creamy milk. Stir to mix together, then sprinkle with more cheese and dot with a few thin flakes of butter and brown quickly in a hot oven.

HARICOT BEAN CROQUETTES

Soak a pint of haricot beans overnight and cook them in the usual way. Drain off the water and rub the beans through a sieve, and put them into a saucepan with two ounces of butter, salt and pepper to taste, a dessertspoonful of finely chopped mint and the same of mild vinegar.

Mix well together and when cold, shape into little balls with floured hands, flatten them, egg-and-breadcrumb them and fry them on each side in butter or other suitable fat.

BEETROOT, AMERICAN FASHION

This is a pleasant way with very small beetroots that can be served whole.

Small beetroots : 1 oz. butter : 1 level dessert-spoonful cornflour : 2 level tablespoonfuls caster sugar : milk.

Cook the beetroots in the usual way, peel them and keep them hot. Make a thick sauce with the butter, sugar, cornflour and sufficient milk, and pour over the beetroots, serve hot.

STEWED BEETROOT

Bake the beetroot (Volume One, page 68) and let it get cold. Then peel it, cut it in slices (reserving a couple) and sprinkle with lemon juice.

Now put the slices into a saucepan with just enough stock to cover them and let them simmer for half an hour.

Now put them into the serving dish and pour over a sauce made by thickening their cooking liquor with a little cream which you have coloured pink by mashing finely with it the two reserved beetroot slices.

Serve hot, sprinkled with chopped parsley.

BRUSSELS SPROUT FRITTERS

For this attractive and unusual way with sprouts you must choose very small tight ones, frozen are fine. Trim them and boil them in salted water for five minutes, then drain them well and season them with salt, pepper and grated nutmeg. For frozen sprouts just defrost and season.

Dip them into coating batter and fry them in hot fat or oil for ten minutes, until their coating is crisp and golden.

Serve sprinkled with grated cheese, and hand a tomato sauce if you wish.

CABBAGE AND MEAT CAKE

Cook and drain the cabbage, squeezing out as much moisture as you can with your hands, and then chop it up roughly. Sprinkle a buttered pie-dish with breadcrumbs and put into it a layer of the cabbage, then a layer of chopped (not minced) cooked meat or slices of cold sausage and repeat these layers until the dish is full, letting the top one be of cabbage. Put three or four fat rashers of bacon on top, and bake in a moderate oven for about forty minutes.

Turn the cake out upside-down to serve to a hungry family.

RED CABBAGE, HOT

Pickled cabbage is one of the Englishman's addictions, but how often, I wonder, does he eat red cabbage hot ?

Red cabbage : 1 cooking apple : 1 tablespoonful chopped onion : 1 oz. butter : 1 saltspoonful salt : a little cayenne pepper : a little nutmeg : 1 dessertspoonful brown sugar : 1 tablespoonful vinegar : 1 pinch powdered cloves : 1 pinch powdered cinnamon.

Slice the red cabbage finely, as if you were going to pickle it, removing any midribs or hard parts, and let the shreds soak in cold water for half an hour. Then put it in handfuls into a saucepan straight out of the bowl with the water still dripping from it. Add the apple, peeled, cored and sliced, the onion, butter and salt, pepper and nutmeg.

Do not add any more liquid, but put the lid on very closely and cook on a low heat for at least an hour, until the cabbage is tender. Now stir in the brown sugar, vinegar, cloves and cinnamon and cook all together for another five minutes or so.

Serve very hot, especially with pork (preferably boiled) or sausages.

FRIED CAULIFLOWER

Cut the raw cauliflower into smallish even-sized flowerets and blanch these in salted water for ten minutes. Drain well and put on to a dish to get cold, placing them apart without touching.

When quite cold, season with a little salt and pepper and dip each separately in flour. Fry in butter on both sides, and serve very hot, sprinkled with a little finely grated cheese, if liked. These are exceptionally good with cutlets or chops.

Or if you prefer something a little more substantial, which could be served as a light separate luncheon course, the floured pieces could be egg-and-breadcrumbed and then fried in deep fat or oil. For this dish the grated cheese is, I think, essential, and should be handed separately.

CAULIFLOWER FRITTERS

Boil a cauliflower but keep the head quite firm, and when it is cold separate the little flowerets and let them lie for half an hour, turning them once or twice, in a mixture of two or three dessertspoonfuls of olive oil and a little lemon juice, with salt, pepper and chopped parsley.

Then drain them, dip them in a good light fritter batter (Volume One, page 106), and fry them crisp and golden in deep fat or oil. Drain them well on kitchen paper, sprinkle them with salt and if they are to make a light separate course, hand a tomato sauce with them.

BRAISED CELERY

Braising Celery is a long and sometimes profitless business. I recommend the following short cut.

Wash and scrape the celery heads and cut them across in three-inch pieces. Dry them well and then fry in a little butter until nicely browned.

Then add a few tablespoonfuls of well-flavoured brown stock or clear gravy, season to taste and baste the celery with this over the heat for a few minutes.

CELERIAC AND SAUSAGE PURÉE

People often ask what the large round whiskery vegetable is that is sometimes seen in the green-grocer's shop. It is the turnip-rooted celery which some think is more delicately flavoured than celery itself.

Peel the celeriac, cut it into slices and cook these in salted water until tender. Cook also separately half as much potato and when they are both done, mash them smoothly together with a piece of butter and a little milk or cream.

Whisk to a very fine purée and then stir in a breakfastcupful of tiny dice of cooked sausage meat and a teaspoonful of chopped parsley. Make as hot as possible, and serve at once.

STUFFED CUCUMBER

Peel the cucumber and cut it exactly in halves lengthways.

Remove the seedy centres carefully with a teaspoon, and fill the cavities with any sort of stuffing you like, perhaps the best being a simple one of buttered breadcrumbs seasoned with salt, pepper, a touch of cayenne and a little onion juice, with chopped parsley if you like.

Bake them in a very little stock in a moderate

oven for about half an hour, stuffed side up-wards, basting them now and then with the liquid that comes from them. Thicken this when they are done, adding a little cream, and pour this pleasant sauce round them.

CORNISH LEEK PIE

4 leeks: bacon rashers: short-crust pastry: thick cream.

Cut the white part of the leeks into quarter-inch slices and take four more thin slices from the green part. Put them into a bowl, cover with boiling water and leave for twenty minutes. Drain off the water, repeat the process, and drain again.

Now put a layer of the leeks into a pie-dish and cover them with thin rashers of bacon, sprinkling with a little pepper. Repeat these leek and bacon layers until the dish is full, and then cover with the pastry. Bake in a moderate oven for an hour and a quarter. Take off the pastry lid and stir in a teacupful of thick cream. Put back the top and put the dish back in the oven for another ten minutes for the contents to heat well through. Serve hot.

JERUSALEM ARTICHOKE CHIPS

A novel change from Chip Potatoes to serve especially with grilled steak or cutlets.

Pare the artichokes and cut them in thin slices, leaving these for an hour in cold water acidu-lated with a little lemon juice.

Take them out, drain them and dry them thoroughly in a clean cloth. Fry them just like the potato chips in deep fat or oil.

JERUSALEM ARTICHOKE MOULD

2 lb. Jerusalem artichokes: $\frac{1}{2}$ pint milk: 2 eggs: salt, pepper and nutmeg: salad.

Pare and boil the artichokes in milk and water, then drain them well and mash them up finely. Mix this purée with the beaten eggs, the milk and the seasoning, pour it into a buttered pudding basin and steam it for an hour.

Serve it when quite cold, turned out and per-haps masked with mayonnaise or salad cream in a bed of green salad.

MUSHROOMS

Smallish flat mushrooms are what you want for these two dishes.

Vienna mushrooms

Leave just a little stalk on the mushrooms and after peeling them dust lightly with seasoned flour. Now dip them thoroughly in beaten egg, roll in fine white breadcrumbs and fry them in deep fat or oil. When they are golden and nearly crisp, serve accompanied by a rather sharp mayonnaise sauce.

Mushrooms in pastry

First fry the mushrooms lightly in butter or bacon fat and at the same time fry some thin slices of streaky bacon cut to much the same size as the mushrooms. Let both get cold and then sandwich a mushroom between two slices of bacon, encase the whole thing in thin pastry, bake until the pastry is cooked and serve hot.

SCALLOPED MUSHROOMS

$\frac{1}{2}$ lb. mushrooms : 1 small onion : 1 oz. butter : milk : breadcrumbs : grated cheese.

Peel and chop up the mushrooms and stew them with the chopped onion in the butter until soft.

Drain off the butter and make with it a thick sauce with an ounce of flour and sufficient milk, and season this to taste with salt, pepper and if you like, a little paprika pepper. Put the mushrooms and onion back into this sauce and cook on for five minutes or so.

Butter some small scallop shells and fill them nearly to the top with the mushroom mixture, sprinkling each afterwards with grated cheese mixed with crumbs first tossed in a little melted butter.

Brown quickly in the oven, and serve as hot as possible. They make a nice savoury or supper dish.

ONION TART

Shortcrust pastry : 3 large onions : bacon : 1 oz. butter : 1 egg : 1 teacupful cream or creamy milk : salt and pepper.

Line a pie-plate or sponge case with your best shortcrust pastry.

Mince up the onions and stew them slowly with the butter and a few very small dice of streaky bacon until tender. Let them cool and then add the beaten egg mixed with the cream or milk and the seasoning which may also include, if you like, a little grated nutmeg.

Mix together well, pour into the tart and bake in a moderate oven for about half an hour, or until the filling is nicely browned.

Serve hot.

ONION RAGOUT

This makes a very pleasant accompaniment to roast lamb or mutton.

2 lb. small onions : 2 oz. butter : 6 cloves : an inch stick of cinnamon : 2 bay leaves : $\frac{1}{2}$ lb. tomatoes : $\frac{1}{2}$ pint good stock.

Fry the onions golden brown in the butter, then add the stock and spices and the fresh or tinned tomatoes rubbed through a sieve to make a purée.

Simmer gently with the lid on for about an hour or until the onions are tender, then remove the spices and serve hot.

POOR MAN'S DUCK

An extremely pleasant dish, especially on a cold day.

6 large onions : 2 lb. cooking apples : 1 breakfastcupful breadcrumbs : 1 level tablespoonful

chopped sage and parsley: 2 tablespoonfuls caster sugar: dripping.

Peel and boil the onions until almost done, then drain and take out the centre of each. Stuff them with the breadcrumb and herb mixture, well seasoned with salt and pepper. Put a small bit of dripping on top of each and transfer them to a hot deep pie dish in which you have first melted a little dripping.

Baste each onion and put round them a mixture of the chopped onion centres and the apples, peeled, cored and sliced. Season with salt and pepper and sprinkle over the sugar. Cover with another pie dish, inverted, and bake in a moderate oven for half an hour.

SPRING ONION TOPS

The more economically minded often think the lengthy green tops usually sold with spring onions are a terrible waste, and wonder whether there is anything to be done with them. As a matter of fact they will make quite a nice savoury.

Put them into enough cold water to cover them, and boil for half an hour.

Then drain them very well indeed and fry slowly until tender in a couple of tablespoonfuls of bacon fat, adding a little pepper if necessary as they cook, and turning them now and then so that they brown evenly.

Then serve them just piled up on buttered toasts.

FRIED PARSLEY

Choose fresh green sprigs, and pick off the thicker stalks which only get tough and string-like if fried with the leaves.

The parsley can be fried in the fat or oil used for the dish which it accompanies, and the best plan is to draw the pan off the heat, with the frying-basket still in it, and leave for three or four minutes to cool a little. Then throw in the parsley and fry it for about a minute, when on drawing out the basket you should find it crisp and a bright green. Drain well before using.

By the way, care should be taken when the parsley is thrown into the fat, as it is very liable to bubble and splash in the frying medium.

PARSNIP CAKES

6 medium-sized parsnips: 1 egg: $\frac{1}{4}$ level tea-spoonful salt: $\frac{3}{4}$ oz. melted butter: a good oz. flour.

Boil the parsnips and mash them up well. Add an egg to this purée and beat until the mixture is light. Now mix in the salt, butter and flour, mix well together again and drop by spoonfuls on to a greased heavy frying-pan, as in making pancakes, and fry brown on both sides.

GREEN PEAS, FRENCH STYLE

Restaurant meals have taught many of us to like petits pois à la française, but not many know how to cook them.

1 lb. shelled new peas : 1 small lettuce : 6 small spring onions : 1 oz. fresh butter : 1 lump of sugar.

Put the cut-up lettuce into a saucepan with the butter and sugar and then add a tablespoonful only of water and the bulbs of the onions and then the peas. Cover and cook over a gentle heat, shaking the pan now and then.

When the peas are done (in about half an hour), pour off what liquid there is into a small pan, and reduce it by quick boiling until it is the right consistency for pouring over the peas, lettuce and onions, and serve at once. If frozen peas are used add them after the other ingredients have been cooking for a quarter of an hour.

For those who do not like the taste of onion, there is much to be said for omitting the spring ones here. The gentle flavour of the peas and lettuce is all that you really want.

BANFFSHIRE POTATOES

Choose some old potatoes all the same size, cut half an inch off the top of each and hollow out the inside leaving a shell of about half an inch thick all round. Cut off also a slice at the bottom so that they will stand up. Fill them with your best minced meat mixture flavoured with onion and moistened with sauce or gravy (or if you are lazy, just fill them with sausagemeat), put on the tops and stand them upright in a baking-tin and bake in a fairly hot oven for an hour or so, basting them the while with melted dripping.

BUTTERED POTATOES

This is really a French dish, pommes Anna, but it might very well be British, for the taste of buttery potatoes is a native one.

Cut some peeled waxy potatoes (large new ones are admirable here) into very thin slices indeed, all as nearly as possible the same thickness, and arrange them in overlapping concentric layers in a shallow round cake tin which has first been well buttered and has a buttered circle of greaseproof paper in the bottom. Each potato layer should be sprinkled with clarified melted butter and with a little salt and pepper.

When the tin is quite full, press the contents tightly down, and cover closely with buttered kitchen foil pressed against the top of the tin to make it as airtight as possible.

Bake on the middle shelf of a moderate oven for an hour, then pour off any surplus butter and turn out the beautifully browned cake upside-down on to the serving dish.

If the first attempt tends to be a little greasy, you may have added too much butter or the potatoes may be too waxy, but this is a case where experience teaches.

CREAMED NEW POTATOES

Cut some boiled new potatoes in slices and put these into a saucepan with half a teacupful of double cream, two ounces of butter, the juice of a small lemon and a seasoning of salt, pepper and grated nutmeg.

Toss well together over a moderate heat until the cream thickens then serve at once, sprinkled if you like with chopped parsley.

POTATO CAKES

An old cook of my childhood used to make some attractive potato cakes like this.

2 lb. potatoes : 2 egg-yolks : 1 oz. butter : 1 teaspoonful cream : salt and pepper.

Steam the potatoes and rub them through a sieve. Mash them finely while still hot and still over a gentle heat mix in the egg-yolks, the butter, cream and seasoning, and if necessary a very little flour to bind the mixture.

Roll this out when cold to half an inch thick, make a crisscross pattern on top with the back of a table knife, cut in suitable pieces and brown them on both sides in a frying-pan greased as for making pancakes.

POTATO BALLS

4 large potatoes : 2 oz. butter : 1 tablespoonful cream : 1 egg : salt and pepper : breadcrumbs : butter for frying.

Cook and mash the potatoes with the butter, salt and pepper, cream and egg-yolk. Make the purée as fine as possible, and shape it with floured hands into small balls about the size of table-tennis balls.

Egg-and-breadcrumb these, using the left-over egg-white to do so, and fry them golden in

butter, rolling them about in the pan so that they colour evenly all over. This quantity of potato should make about a dozen balls.

POTATO FRITTERS

An old-fashioned way of Scottish origin.

Half-cook six large potatoes, and cut them in eighth of an inch-thick slices. While these are cooling, beat up two eggs with a tablespoonful each of breadcrumbs and grated lean ham or bacon, and when quite cold coat each slice on both sides with this mixture and fry in deep oil.

POTATOES AND LEMON

Scrape and half-cook some small new potatoes in salted water, then pour all the water away except enough just to cover them.

Into this squeeze the juice of a lemon, and finish cooking them in this.

When they are done, drain them well, pour over them some melted butter and, just as they leave the kitchen, sprinkle them with freshly chopped parsley.

POTATO MERINGUES

4 good-sized potatoes : $\frac{1}{2}$ oz. melted butter : 2 tablespoonfuls cream : 1 slightly beaten egg-yolk : 1 egg-white : salt, pepper and grated nutmeg.

Bake the potatoes in their jackets and mash up the pulp finely. Mix with it the butter, cream, egg-yolk and seasonings and cook gently for three minutes, stirring all the time.

Take the pan off the heat and add the well-whisked egg-white by degrees. Then shape the mixture between two spoons into meringue shapes and lay them on a buttered baking-sheet.

Bake them in a moderate oven until they are a delicate brown, and serve immediately.

POTATO PUFF

An adoption from America, I think, but no doubt arrived there originally from Europe. Any new way with potato is always welcomed.

1 breakfastcupful cold mashed potato : 2 tablespoonfuls melted butter : 2 whisked eggs : 1 teacupful milk or thin cream : salt and pepper.

Beat the potato and butter to a white creamy mixture, and then add the eggs, the seasoning and the milk or, better, cream.

Beat all together thoroughly, and then turn the mixture into a deep fireproof dish and bake in a moderately hot oven until browned.

If this is done properly, the mixture turns out very light and puffy, and is specially good with roast chicken or veal.

SALSIFY OYSTERS

Cook (Volume One, page 77) and mash up enough salsify to give two breakfastcupfuls and add to this a beaten egg, half a level teaspoonful of salt, half an ounce of melted butter and a little anchovy essence.

Shape with floured hands into small round flat cakes, about the size of a large oyster, dust them with fine breadcrumbs and fry them in butter until browned on both sides, which will take about ten minutes.

SPINACH PANCAKE

The simplest way is to mix some finely chopped cooked and well dried spinach with an equal amount of unsweetened pancake batter, seasoning rather highly and adding a little nutmeg, and to cook pancakes made with this mixture in the usual way, serving them with melted butter and grated cheese.

But it is nicer and more decorative to spread the cooked seasoned spinach mixture on thin cooked pancakes and to pile these on top of each other until you have a heap of three or four. When the pile is finished, sprinkle it with melted butter and grated cheese, and brown in the oven. Cut down in slices like a cake to serve, with more cheese and melted butter handed separately.

TOMATO AND ONION PIE

A country dish first encountered very many years ago in a gamekeeper's cottage in Somerset.

Peel a couple of large onions, put them into boiling water, and leave them there for two or three hours. Then drain, dry and slice them and fry them lightly in an ounce of butter.

Spinach pancake

Butter a fireproof dish and fill it with alternate layers of peeled sliced tomatoes and onions, seasoning each layer with salt and pepper and sprinkling with a few breadcrumbs.

Finish with a good layer of crumbs, dot with butter and bake in a moderate oven for about an hour.

To make a really authentic dish of it, surmount the top when cooked with fried or poached eggs.

TOMATO JELLY

A useful trick learned from America is the tomato jelly which is so useful for garnishing salads.

Quarter some ripe tomatoes and put them, skin and all, into a saucepan with a clove, a very small teaspoonful of chopped onion, salt, pepper, a pinch of sugar and a drop of tarragon vinegar if you like it.

Do not add any liquid, but put on the lid and stew very gently until the tomatoes are tender. Then take out the clove and press, not rub, the rest through a fine sieve or cloth or muslin.

To every pint of the juice thus obtained add half an ounce of powdered gelatine (a little more in hot weather and if there is no refrigerator handy), stir until it begins to cool, and let it set in the coldest place you have.

It can be moulded in a border or in small cups for use in containing or surrounding the salad of your choice. A few chopped stuffed or plain green olives can be added to the mixture when it is on the point of setting.

Salads

Possibly due to the increasing benefits of commercial and domestic refrigeration, salads are eaten more than ever before in this country. A number of different mixtures are given here, as well as a note on salad dressings and how they can be varied.

OIL AND VINEGAR DRESSING (FRENCH DRESSING) (see Volume One, page 80)

The variations given here are in respect of a teacupful of the plain dressing. All spoonfuls are level.

Anchovy dressing (for Fish Salads): add two teaspoonfuls of anchovy paste, creamed, and three teaspoonfuls each of chopped parsley and onion.

Cheese and egg dressing: add three teaspoonfuls each of chopped parsley and sweet red peppers, three tablespoonfuls chopped Cheddar cheese and one chopped hard-boiled egg.

Chutney dressing: add three dessertspoonfuls of chopped chutney.

Cumberland dressing: make the dressing with lemon juice instead of vinegar and add three teaspoonfuls each of red currant jelly and thick cream and a quarter of a teaspoonful of grated lemon rind.

Horseradish dressing: add three teaspoonfuls of scraped or grated horseradish.

Lemon or grapefruit dressing: use lemon or grapefruit juice instead of vinegar.

Mint dressing: add three teaspoonfuls of chopped fresh mint.

Tomato dressing: add a teaspoonful of strained tomato juice and a little onion juice.

MAYONNAISE DRESSING
(see Volume One, page 26)

Quantities for one teacupful of the dressing. All spoonfuls level.

Cheese mayonnaise: mix three teaspoonfuls of thin cream with the mayonnaise and fold in a third of a breakfastcupful of grated cheese, seasoning with salt and pepper.

Chutney mayonnaise: add three teaspoonfuls of chopped chutney.

Cream mayonnaise: fold in a third of a breakfastcupful of well-whipped thick cream.

Ham mayonnaise: add half a teacupful of tomato juice and three dessertspoonfuls of chopped ham.

Mustard cream mayonnaise: add three tablespoonfuls of French or mild English mustard and fold in a teacupful of whipped cream.

Pickle mayonnaise: add a teaspoonful and a half each of ketchup and minced parsley and then add three teaspoonfuls each of minced sweet pickle, pickled gherkin and pickled beetroot.

Red mayonnaise: colour to taste with tinned tomato purée or paste.

Savoury mayonnaise: (1) add an eighth of a teaspoonful each of dry mustard, paprika pepper and Worcestershire sauce. (2) Add three teaspoonfuls each of finely chopped green olives and pickles.

APPLE AND BEETROOT SALAD

Dice a large cooked beetroot, two large cooked waxy potatoes and two large peeled and cored apples. Season with salt and pepper and dress with mayonnaise. Stir in a couple of teaspoonfuls of capers if you like the taste.

APPLE AND CELERY SALAD

Core and scoop out the insides of red-skinned apples, one for each person, and rub the inside with a cut lemon to prevent discolouration. Now cut the apple flesh, and as much celery into small pieces, dress these with mayonnaise and after well mixing together, fill the apples with this mixture. Serve accompanied by a nice lettuce leaf or two, or some sprigs of watercress.

APPLE AND TOMATO SALAD

Take equal quantities of quartered peeled ripe tomatoes and quartered peeled and cored des-

sert apples, and put them into a salad bowl with a sprinkling of a teaspoonful of caster sugar and a tiny pinch of salt. Then dress with mayonnaise.

ARTICHOKE AND POTATO SALAD

Cut two cooked Jerusalem artichokes (Volume One, page 68), two potatoes, and a raw peeled and cored apple into smallish dice, and then slice in half a head of celery. Sprinkle with a little chopped parsley, dress with mayonnaise and serve on a bed of watercress.

ASPARAGUS SALAD

Cold cooked or tinned asparagus tips are arranged in lettuce leaves, coated with mayonnaise and sprinkled lastly with chopped parsley.

MIXED BEAN SALAD

Mix cold haricot beans with cold French or runner beans cut in diamond shapes and dress with French dressing or mayonnaise. If liked, a little chopped parsley or onion or both may be added, also some shreds of peeled tomato flesh.

BEETROOT AND CHICORY SALAD

Mix diced cooked beetroot with sliced chicory and dress with mayonnaise flavoured with a little mustard. This can be served in a border of potato salad, if wished.

BEETROOT AND HORSERADISH SALAD

Chop up a cooked beetroot coarsely and mix it in a salad bowl with a small handful of grated horseradish. Just cover with boiling tarragon vinegar, set aside for at least twelve hours then drain and serve in a bed of green salad.

BEETROOT AND MINT SALAD

Arrange thin slices of cooked beetroot on lettuce, sprinkle with finely chopped mint and pour mayonnaise over them.

BROAD BEAN SALAD

Dress cold young broad beans with French dressing, and sprinkle with parsley. Serve decorated with roughly sieved hard-boiled egg-yolks and chopped whites.

CAULIFLOWER SALAD

Cook the cauliflowerets so that they are still quite firm, then drain them and let them get cold. Dress them with mayonnaise to which you have added a little finely minced fresh mint. A border of sliced tomatoes might be permitted.

CELERY AND APPLE SALAD

Cut some celery and peeled and cored apples into thin short strips, and mix and dress them with mayonnaise flavoured with tomato sauce or purée.

CHEESE AND TOMATO SALAD

Skin and cut up three tomatoes and mix them with two small lettuces, shredded. Mix with two ounces of grated cheese and dress with mayonnaise or French dressing.

CHICKEN SALAD

Mix together two breakfastcupfuls of diced cold chicken, a teacupful each of chopped celery and diced cucumber and two tablespoonfuls of capers. Toss all together and moisten with mayonnaise.

DUTCH CHEESE SALAD

Sprinkle a green salad with Dutch cheese cut into small bits, and moisten with French dressing. Alternatively cook some peas and allow to become cold. Mix with cubed Dutch cheese and a few spring onions. Cut into rings and serve garnished with lettuce.

ENGLISH SALAD

Mix together two shredded lettuces, a bunch of watercress, a handful of mustard and cress, a bunch of sliced radishes and a few finely sliced spring onions. Dress with oil and vinegar.

ENGLISH WINTER SALAD

Mix together dice of cooked potato, carrot and turnip and raw apple and celery. Moisten with mayonnaise to which you have added a little onion juice.

FARMHOUSE SALAD

Mix together pickled red cabbage, sliced cold potatoes and raw celery in the proportions you like, and dress with mayonnaise.

FRENCH BEAN AND APPLE SALAD

Mix together two and a half breakfastcupfuls of cooked and sliced French (or runner) beans, half a teacupful of diced peeled and cored apple, a teacupful of the white heart of a raw cabbage and enough mayonnaise to moisten. Serve on a green salad.

GREEN PEA SALAD

Simply dress the cold green peas with mayonnaise mixed with lightly whipped cream and flavoured with the merest touch of onion juice, and serve with a few lettuce heart leaves. Sprinkle with a very little chopped mint, if you like.

LETTUCE WITH SOUR CREAM DRESSING

Make a lettuce salad in the usual way and dress it with half a pint of sour or cultured cream

mixed with a teaspoonful and a half of vinegar and one of caster sugar. Serve decorated with slices of hard-boiled egg.

MACEDOINE SALAD

Cut into small pieces a cooked beetroot, some cold French or runner beans, two ounces of asparagus tips, cooked or tinned, two table-spoonfuls of cooked green peas, a small cold boiled carrot and a small head of celery. Mix together and dress with mayonnaise.

POTATO AND BACON SALAD

Unusual but very good. While they are still hot peel and cut up into small pieces some new or waxy potatoes boiled in their skins. Mix them with a few rashers of fat bacon crisply fried and cut in small pieces. Add the fat from the frying. Mix in a warm salad bowl, adding a little vinegar and sprinkling with chopped parsley and chives or the green part of young spring onions. Serve warm.

POTATO AND ANCHOVY SALAD

Make a potato salad as on page 213 and add to it before dressing half a dozen or so anchovy fillets in oil cut in small bits.

BAKED POTATO SALAD

Bake a potato for each person in its jacket, cut

them in halves lengthways, scoop out the inside as much in one piece as possible, and when cold cut into small dice. Mix these with the same quantity of peeled and cored apple, also diced, season with salt and pepper, dress with mayonnaise and heap back into the potato cases, sprinkling the tops with chopped parsley on serving. This salad can be varied by using celery or tomatoes instead of apple.

POTATO AND WATERCRESS SALAD

Add to a plain potato salad a handful of watercress leaves. Dress with mayonnaise and sprinkle with chopped parsley and hard-boiled egg.

POTATO SALAD

Boil or steam the potatoes, as waxy as possible, in their skins and peel them while they are still hot. Cut them in slices and dress them at once with a little oil-and-vinegar. Let them get cold and then drain away any of the dressing, sprinkle the potatoes with finely chopped spring onions or chives or spring onion green, dress them with mayonnaise and serve sprinkled with chopped parsley.

RED CABBAGE SALAD

Shred a small red cabbage finely and leave the shreds to soak for about six hours in a mixture of half water and half vinegar. Then drain well and mix with a peeled and cored apple cut in very small dice. Put this salad in the centre of a border of potato salad and serve.

SALSIFY SALAD

Slice the cold cooked salsify (Volume One, page 77) and dress it with mayonnaise flavoured with a little anchovy essence to which chopped parsley has been added.

SWEET CORN SALAD

Drain thoroughly two breakfastcupfuls of tinned sweet corn and season with mustard and onion juice. Let it lie for an hour sprinkled well with French dressing, then drain it again and serve on lettuce leaves. You may care to add diced cucumber.

TOMATO SALAD (FROZEN)

Take two breakfastcupfuls of cold stewed or tinned tomatoes and sweeten with three level dessertspoonfuls of caster sugar. Season with salt and pepper, rub through a sieve and freeze in small moulds in the refrigerator. Turn out when frozen and serve on lettuce leaves, with mayonnaise handed separately.

TOMATO SALAD, STUFFED

Scoop out the centres of some large ripe tomatoes, season the inside lightly with salt and pepper and fill them with green pea salad (page 212) or with apple and celery chopped with the tomato flesh and dressed with mayonnaise.

STUFFED TOMATOES

6 large ripe tomatoes: 6 tablespoonfuls of plainly cooked or savoury rice: (if plain rice, a small onion is needed): 3 or 4 mushrooms: butter.

Peel and cut the mushrooms into small thin strips and fry them lightly with the finely chopped onion. Mix the chopped insides of the tomatoes with the rice, mushrooms and onion, season with salt and plenty of freshly-ground black pepper and fill up the tomato shells with the mixture. Sprinkle the top with buttered crumbs and bake for a quarter of an hour or so in a moderate oven. Grated cheese may be added to the crumbs, if liked.

For Cold Stuffed Tomatoes see under Salads, on page 78.

TUNA FISH SALAD

Mix drained flakes of tinned tuna fish with an equal amount of tomato, red flesh only. Sprinkle with a finely chopped spring onion or two and moisten with a French dressing made with the oil from the tin.

WATERCRESS SALAD

Moisten the watercress with a French dressing in which you have used lemon juice instead of vinegar, or if you prefer arrange the watercress in the salad bowl, sprinkle it with beetroot cut in small thin strips and dress with a mayonnaise made with lemon juice instead of vinegar.

WHITE SALAD

Slice the white part of a head of celery and four or five cold new potatoes. Mix these with some just cooked but cold sprigs of cauliflower and a little chopped spring onion. Moisten with a creamy-white mayonnaise. Turn on to a bed of lettuce and decorate with a few cooked cauli-flowerets kept back for the purpose.

YORKSHIRE SALAD

Chop up finely some lettuce, spring onions and mint, put them into a salad bowl and add granulated sugar and vinegar to taste. Leave until the sugar has dissolved, and then serve after draining

Note. Garlic-fanciers may note that all suitable salads can be improved to meet their taste by first rubbing the bottom and sides of the salad bowl, before operations begin, with a cut clove of it.

Eggs

A good deal of prominence has been given to egg cookery, because this commodity is of such general use today when families tend to be small and there are so many people living alone or in very small groups, where quickness in preparing food is so much desired. It is with such people in mind that the section on omelettes has been prepared, as giving them a chance to vary a simply made dish in a large number of simple ways. More substantial dishes have not been forgotten, as witness the Glasgow eggs, eggs in onion, or tomato, nor the less usual kind like egg kromeskies or fried poached egg, while the children may well discover a new favourite in ox eyes.

OMELETTES

Although the soufflé omelette (see Volume One, page 82) is the true British version, the so-called French omelette has ousted it from the kitchen here, probably because it is much easier to make and certainly susceptible to more variation. The art of making this omelette, like kneading of dough, is one which is difficult to describe in writing, but can be learned in a minute from anyone who possesses it already. So get your most omelette-minded friend to show you.

It is important to use a heavy pan for frying omelettes, and it should be the right size for the number of eggs used. For an omelette of three eggs, which is enough for two, the outside measurement should be six or seven inches; for six eggs nearly double that size. Start with three eggs and try. Second, the eggs should not be beaten too much. All you want to do is to beat them lightly with a fork so that the yolks and whites are just mixed, without the least suspicion of froth. Only do this immediately before you want to cook them. If you like a light texture in your omelette, a little thin cream or milk can now be added, in the proportion of a tablespoonful for three eggs. Third, use butter, preferably clarified, for the sake of the flavour, and see that the right amount is used, a little over half an ounce for each egg. Remember that the omelette has to be cooked quickly so a good heat will be needed, for in the French omelette you are aiming at the consistence of scrambled egg inside with an outside solid enough to allow the omelette to be folded. This process should not take more than two and a half minutes.

The actual cooking is done like this. Beat the eggs as described above and unless the omelette is to be a sweet one, season with salt and pepper and stir in the cream or milk if desired. Put the butter in the cold pan on the heat, and as it melts move the pan to and fro so that it coats the bottom and a little way up the sides of the pan. When it begins to colour and smells slightly nutty, pour the eggs all at once into the middle. With the left hand keep shaking the pan and at the same time, with the right, stir the eggs with a fork as in making scrambled egg, working away from the sides towards the middle. Do not hurry over this, and after a few seconds give the pan a shaking backwards and forwards, holding it flat, to stop the mixture from sticking. As soon as the centre of the omelette looks scrambled enough, leave the pan stationary on the heat for four or five seconds for the bottom to brown slightly. Then, if you can get somebody to show you how, roll the omelette over on itself to fold it in two. Or with infinite care fold it from opposite sides on to the middle with a wide palette knife. Then slip it off on to your hot dish or plate, upside down so that the browned surface comes on top.

This is how a plain omelette is made, but there are a very large number of variations invented by the French, some in which the extra ingredients are first mixed with the beaten eggs and others where a stuffing is made which is spread on the cooked omelette before it is folded. The simplest of these is what the English call a Savoury Omelette, and this is made by mixing with the uncooked eggs a mixture of chopped parsley, mixed herbs and either chopped onion, onion green or chives, if you have the last. This is merely a modest version of the French omelette aux fines herbes in which the herbs are equal parts of finely chopped parsley, chervil, chives and tarragon, a savoury mixture indeed. Other variations follow in alphabetical order.

Asparagus omelette: mix cooked or tinned asparagus tips with the uncooked eggs and sprinkle the cooked omelette with grated cheese.

Omelette aux Anchois: mix with the uncooked eggs a little anchovy essence and a few finely chopped anchovy fillets.

Omelette Andalouse: stuff the cooked omelette with roughly chopped stewed tomatoes and sweet red peppers, and serve surrounded by fried onion rings.

Omelette Bonne Femme: mix with the uncooked eggs, small dice of green bacon and minced mushrooms both previously fried lightly in butter with some thinly sliced onions, all well drained.

Omelette Boulonnaise: stuff the cooked omelette with poached soft herrings' roes bound with maître d'hôtel butter, and pour more of this butter, melted, round it.

Omelette Bretonne: mix with the uncooked eggs thinly-cut onion and the white part of leek, both first stewed in butter with some minced mushrooms.

Omelette aux Champignons: mix with the uncooked eggs lightly fried chopped mushrooms. Stuff also with stewed mushrooms if you wish.

Omelette aux Crevettes: stuff the cooked omelette with shrimps bound with shrimp sauce.

Omelette Espagnole: mix with the uncooked eggs, roughly chopped tomatoes, thin strips of onion and of sweet red peppers, all first stewed in butter or olive oil or a mixture of the two.

Omelette Grand Mère: mix with the un-cooked eggs some chopped parsley and tiny dice of bread fried crisply at the last moment.

Omelette Hollandaise: mix with the un-cooked eggs some thin slices of smoked salmon stiffened in butter, and pour Hollandaise sauce round the omelette when it is cooked.

Omelette au Jambon: mix with the uncooked eggs pieces of ham lightly fried in butter. Decorate the top with strips of ham.

Omelette au Kari: fry some chopped onion golden-brown in the butter, season with curry powder and add a spoonful of Béchamel sauce. Stuff the cooked omelette with this and pour round it, if you like, a little curry sauce.

Omelette Lyonnaise: mix with the uncooked eggs minced onions fried in butter and serve with a heap of these on top.

Omelette Portugaise: stuff with roughly chopped stewed tomatoes and serve with a tomato sauce poured round it.

Omelette au Thon: mix with the uncooked eggs well-drained dice of tinned tuna fish. When the omelette is cooked, sprinkle it with melted anchovy butter.

Cheese omelette: mix grated cheese with the uncooked eggs in the proportion you like, sprinkle the cooked omelette with a little melted butter and hand more grated cheese with it.

Potato omelette: mix with the uncooked eggs small dice of potato first fried raw in butter.

Sausage omelette: Grill four chipolata saus-ages, drain them, keep them hot and use them to stuff a plain omelette. Serve surrounded by tomato sauce.

SWEET OMELETTES

Sweet omelettes are made in exactly the same way, a pinch of caster sugar and a very small pinch of salt being added to the beaten eggs.

Jam omelette: fold into the cooked ome-lettes some warmed jam, and on serving sprinkle the top with icing sugar.

Christmas omelette: add a very little rum to the uncooked eggs, stuff the cooked omelette with warmed mincemeat, pour over a liqueur-glassful of warmed rum or brandy, and set it alight as it comes to table.

Kirsch omelette: add a little Kirsch to the un-cooked eggs, pour some warmed Kirsch over the cooked omelette and set it alight.

Peach omelette: stuff the cooked omelette with diced tinned peaches heated up in a little of their syrup flavoured with Maraschino or Kirsch.

Rum omelette: make as Kirsch omelette, using rum instead.

Other egg dishes

CHEESE EGG BALLS

4 hard-boiled eggs: 2 oz. breadcrumbs: 2 teaspoonfuls finely chopped parsley: 1 oz. grated cheese: salt, pepper and a touch of cayenne pepper: 1 egg: milk.

Chop up the hard-boiled eggs finely and mix them with the breadcrumbs slightly moistened with a little milk, the parsley, cheese and seasonings.

Bind with a beaten egg, roll into balls in browned breadcrumbs and fry golden in deep fat or oil.

Serve with tomato sauce poured round, not over, them, and garnish with fried parsley.

CHEESE EGGS

Line a buttered shallow fireproof dish with thin slices of cheese, preferably Gruyère. Break some eggs over this, keeping the yolks intact and season them with salt and white pepper.

Add a tablespoonful or two of cream, and sprinkle with more of the cheese, grated this time.

Now sprinkle with buttered crumbs and bake in a hot oven for about ten minutes.

CURRIED SCRAMBLED EGGS

To each egg allow a dessertspoonful of chopped onion and a quarter of a large teaspoonful of curry powder.

Fry the onion in butter until golden, then add the curry powder with a little salt to taste and cook gently together for three or four minutes with the lid on.

Add a bit more butter and then the lightly beaten eggs, and scramble in the usual way. Serve in a border of plainly boiled rice if a light dish is wanted, or on buttered toasts as a savoury.

CURRIED TOMATO EGGS

Peel and chop roughly equal quantities of tomatoes and onions, and stew these slowly in a little bacon fat until you have a thick soft purée, which you must then season to taste with salt.

Now for every pound of the mixed vegetables used allow a dessertspoonful of curry powder (or more if you like, but its flavour must not predominate) and just a little more fat. Stir this into the purée, mixing well.

Cook on gently for a quarter of an hour and then off the heat break in an egg for each person, stirring with a fork to mix. Go on stirring and beating until the eggs are cooked and the resulting purée is smooth and thick and in which neither onion, tomato or egg are separately visible. It must be served very hot indeed, and can be garnished with sippets of fried bread or indeed accompanied by a dish of rice.

EGG AND HAM TARTLETS

½ lb. short crust paste : 4 oz. cooked ham or bacon : 3 hard-boiled eggs : 3 raw egg-yolks : cream : salt, pepper and nutmeg.

Line a dozen small tartlet tins with the paste.

Mince finely the ham and hard-boiled eggs and bind this mixture, after seasoning with salt, pepper and grated nutmeg, with the raw egg-yolks mixed with a little cream. Chopped parsley may be introduced, if wished. Bake in a moderate oven until the pastry is cooked and the contents set. Serve them hot, accompanied by a tomato sauce handed separately.

EGG AND MINT PIE

An eggy version of a popular Yorkshire mint turnover.

Line a pie-plate or sponge tin with short crust paste, and spread the bottom with cream or cottage cheese. Break four eggs on to this so that the yolks are intact and fairly evenly apart.

Sprinkle thickly with fresh chopped mint, cover with a thin pastry top, bake in a hottish oven until the pastry is cooked. Serve cold.

EGGS IN ONIONS

4 large onions : 1 oz. grated cheese : 4 eggs : salt and pepper : butter.

Skin the onions, which must each be large enough to hold an egg, and boil them until just tender in salted water. Drain well, cut a slice off the top of each and scoop out most of the centre, leaving enough room for the egg.

Chop up the pulp that has been withdrawn, season it with salt and pepper and mix with the grated cheese. Now put four heaps of this on a buttered shallow fireproof dish, place an onion on top of each of these and season the cavity with salt, pepper, and a very small bit of butter.

Slip a whole egg into each, sprinkle the top with more grated cheese and dot with a flake of butter. Bake in a moderate oven until the eggs are nicely set.

EGG SANDWICH FILLINGS

To chopped hard-boiled egg add :

Minced onion and mayonnaise flavoured with mustard.

Minced celery and tinned sweet red pepper bound with mayonnaise.

Chopped drained mixed pickles and mayonnaise.

Chopped stuffed olives and mayonnaise.

Diced crisply-fried bacon or chopped boiled ham and mayonnaise.

Chopped watercress or cucumber and mayonnaise.

Grated cheese mixed to a paste with butter and a little mustard.

Chopped chutney.

Chopped pickled gherkins.

Grated horseradish, a spot of vinegar and some thick cream.

EGG SAVOURY

The attraction of this very simple savoury lies in the fact that the flavour of none of the ingredients must predominate. A little experiment will ensure this.

For a couple of hard-boiled eggs, chop up a very small onion and fry it golden in a little butter. To this add a finely chopped anchovy fillet and then the finely chopped eggs. Cook on a few minutes together to get them all really hot all through, and pile up on hot buttered toasts.

EGGS IN TOMATOES

Cut a slice from the stem end of a large firm, ripe tomato, scoop out the core and surrounding pulp so that only the flesh remains inside the skin. Sprinkle the inside with salt and pepper and break in a whole egg.

Sprinkle this very lightly indeed with more salt and pepper, coat the surface of the egg with buttered crumbs, and bake in a moderate oven until the white is firm. It will take about ten minutes. Serve one for each person as quickly as you can, for the egg will go on cooking a bit in the tomato and may set too hard.

FRIED EGGS WITH ANCHOVY

Fry some eggs in butter so that the whites are folded over the yolks and are nice and crisp.

Have ready some pieces of fried bread and on each spread a layer of minced anchovies or

anchovy paste mixed with chopped parsley.

Serve an egg on each of these, sprinkling it as it goes to table with plenty of freshly-ground black pepper.

FRIED POACHED EGGS

Poach lightly as many eggs as you want, and when they are quite cold, trim them neatly.

Dip each in coating batter (Volume One, page 103) and drop each carefully into deep hot fat or oil.

Fry crisp and golden, drain on kitchen paper and serve with a tomato sauce.

GLASGOW EGGS

A curious example of our ancestors liking for the mixture of curry and cheese, and pleasant to those who like strongish flavours.

1 tablespoonful butter : 1 tablespoonful milk : 4 oz. flaked cooked white fish : 1 teaspoonful each of curry powder and Worcestershire sauce : $\frac{1}{2}$ teaspoonful chopped parsley : 3 eggs : salt and pepper : grated cheese.

Melt the butter in a saucepan and add the milk, fish, curry powder and sauce, parsley and seasoning.

Cook together for a few minutes, stirring with a fork, then add the lightly beaten eggs and scramble all together.

When nearly of the right consistency to serve, turn the mixture into a shallow fireproof dish, sprinkle the top with the cheese, and brown very quickly under the grill.

OX-EYES

Victorian children seem to have liked these for breakfast.

Toast some bread and stamp out rounds of it, cutting out the centres to form a ring. Butter each ring and place them in a well-buttered fireproof dish side by side. Break an egg carefully into each centre, sprinkle with salt and pepper and pour about a dessertspoonful of cream or a little melted butter over each egg. Bake in a rather slow oven until the white is set, about ten minutes. Grated cheese may be added for adults.

SAVOURY BAKED EGGS

These little moulds are pretty and attractive, whether served as a savoury or a breakfast or supper dish.

Chop up finely a quarter of a pound of lean cooked ham and mix it with a dessertspoonful of chopped parsley. Butter thickly six small deep patty pans or dariole moulds, and scatter some of the ham mixture into each, shaking it about so that the bottom and sides are well coated. Tap out any loose bits of the mixture.

Now break an egg carefully into each mould, sprinkle with salt and a touch of cayenne pepper, and put a small flake of butter on top.

Bake in a pan of hot water in a moderate oven until the egg is set, for ten minutes or so, then turn out upside-down on small rounds of buttered toast.

SAVOURY EGG PIE

Line a buttered pie dish with breadcrumbs seasoned with salt and pepper. Cover with a layer of sliced peeled tomatoes and on these spread a thin layer of mashed potato.

Break over this four eggs, spacing them evenly, sprinkle them with chopped capers, then more breadcrumbs and another layer of tomato slices and of mashed potato.

Continue until the dish is full, leaving the last layer of breadcrumbs. Dot this with thin flakes of butter and bake in a hot oven for about twenty minutes.

EGG KROMESKIS

Chop up three hard-boiled eggs rather coarsely, mix them with chopped ham or tongue and if you like, a little chopped parsley and bind with a thick white sauce.

Make half a dozen very thin small pancakes, spread some of the mixture on each, roll up and seal the ends and joins with white of egg.

Dip them carefully into your best coating batter (Volume One, page 103) and fry them golden in deep fat or oil.

See also Chicken Kromeskis, page 189.

Puddings

This is a brief selection to add to the puddings already given in Volume One, mostly old friends of my generation which I would like to pass on to those who have probably never tasted them, in particular the delights of the Guards pudding, the Kentish apple pie with its unusual layer of cheese and the Duke of Cambridge tart with its egg-coated bed of candied peel or crystallised fruit. American importations are here too for the experimentalists, the world-known strawberry shortcake sweet delicacy. Switzerland contributes a cream cheese tartlet and a Bavarian Charlotte encased in circles of Swiss roll, France the exquisite simplicity of buttered apples and pears, and Italy a fine luscious dish of cherries and red wine.

As a personal footnote to the recipe for apple pie in Volume One I should like to say that the most fragrant results can be obtained if a few slices of ripe quince are added to the apple or if immediately before the pastry crust is put on the top of the pie a layer of red rose petals is inserted or, here and there, a few peach leaves.

APPLE AMBER

2 lb. cooking apples : sugar to taste : 2–3 eggs : 1 lemon : 1 oz. butter : $\frac{1}{4}$ lb. short crust pastry.

Line a pie dish with the pastry (see page 84).

Stew the peeled, cored and sliced apples with the rind and juice of the lemon, adding the sugar and butter, and very little water indeed. Rub through a hair or nylon sieve when done, add the egg-yolks, stirring together well, and then pour the mixture into the pie dish. Bake in a moderate oven until the pastry is cooked and the contents of the pie firm, and then whisk the egg-whites stiffly. Fold in a tablespoonful of caster sugar, and pile this meringue mixture on top of the pudding. Sprinkle some more caster sugar over it and stick in a few blanched sweet almonds, whole or halved lengthways, if you like. Bake in a very cool oven until the topping is fawn-coloured and crisp, and serve hot or cold. Some like to add a very little red vegetable colouring to the whisked whites, which gives the meringue a pretty mottled pink and white effect.

TOFFEE APPLE PUDDING

$\frac{1}{2}$ lb. flour : 6 oz. shredded suet : $1\frac{1}{2}$ lb. cooking apples : 6 teaspoonfuls brown sugar and 2 oz. butter and 2 oz. brown sugar extra.

Smear thickly a pie-dish with the two ounces of butter and brown sugar mixed well together, and line this with thin suet crust. Put in the peeled, cored and cut-up apples, add the six tablespoonfuls of sugar, and cover with the rest of the suet crust.

Bake in a moderate oven for an hour and a quarter, and turn out carefully. It will be coated with a delicious toffee-like sauce.

APPLE MERINGUES

These are highly decorative and exciting.

6 even-sized apples : sugar syrup : 2 whites of egg : 1 oz. caster sugar : sweet almonds.

Core and peel the apples and cook them whole in sugar syrup (sugar and water) until only just tender. Transfer them from the syrup to a baking-tin or shallow fireproof dish and when they are cold cover them with a meringue made in the usual way (Volume One, page 116) but with two egg-whites and one ounce of caster sugar. When coated sprinkle them with more sugar and stick long splinters of blanched sweet almonds all over them. Brown them in a very moderate oven and serve them with the syrup thickened by rapid boilings poured round them.

FRUIT MERINGUE

This mixture can be used to spread over a pie-dish of fruit which if cooked must be first allowed to go cold. It is smoothed over the top, dusted with icing sugar and baked in a very cool oven for about two hours until crisp and fawn-coloured.

Meringues can of course be squeezed out of a forcing-bag into any shapes you like, and baked in the same way.

APPLES IN SHERRY

5 medium-sized cooking apples : blanched sweet almonds : ½ lb. granulated sugar : 5 oz. brown sugar : 1 teacupful sherry : cream.

Peel and core the apples and cut them in halves lengthways. Stick the rounded side all over with halved or splintered blanched almonds and arrange them side by side in a shallow fireproof dish with a lid.

Make a syrup with the sugars and sherry and pour this boiling hot over the apples. Put the lid on tightly and bake in a moderate oven until the

Apple meringue

apples are tender, basting several times during their cooking.

Take off the lid for the last twenty minutes and go on basting, so that the apples will be glazed with the syrup. Serve hot or cold, with cream.

BAKED BANANAS

6 bananas : 1 teacupful orange juice : 3 table-spoonfuls brown sugar : 1 breakfastcupful grated fresh or desiccated coconut.

Cut the bananas in halves lengthways after peeling them. Arrange them side by side in a buttered fireproof dish and pour over them the orange juice and sugar. Sprinkle with the coconut and bake in a moderate oven for ten minutes.

Hand whipped cream.

BANANA MOULD

Sweets of this kind are a little troublesome to make, but if you have a refrigerator you will be spared some of the bother.

3 ripe but not over-ripe bananas : 1 pint lemon or orange jelly : glacé cherries and either angelica or pistachio nuts for decoration.

Set a quarter-inch layer of clear jelly in the bottom of a border mould and decorate with the fruit and nuts. Set this in place with a few drops of jelly and arrange a layer of banana slices on top, setting these in place with jelly also. Now pour over enough liquid jelly, while cold, to cover the bananas, and repeat these layers, putting the mould each time in the refrigerator until each new layer is set, until the mould is full. Leave the top layer to set and when ready, turn out and fill the centre with whipped cream or with one of the creams described on page 112 of Volume One.

BAVARIAN CHARLOTTE

A simple form of Charlotte Russe which is unusually attractive to look at and delicious to eat. It may be made with either of the last two varieties of Creams on page 114 of Volume One. This is the Bavarois specially recommended here.

4 yolks of eggs : 1 pint milk : ½ pint whipped cream : ½ lb. caster sugar : ¼ oz. gelatine : vanilla essence. Also 1 red jam Swiss roll.

Dissolve the gelatine in a little warm water and beat the sugar with the egg-yolks and add vanilla to taste and a pinch of salt. Heat up the milk and add to the egg mixture, stirring well. Heat nearly to boiling point but not quite and strain through a sieve. Now add the dissolved gelatine slowly by degrees, stirring all the time, and when the mixture begins to set, stir in the whipped cream.

Meanwhile you will have lined the top and sides of a pudding-basin with thin slices of the jam roll pressed tightly together so as to contain the cream. Pour this in carefully without disturbing the slices, and leave to set. Turn out to serve accompanied by a sauceboat of red jam or fruit sauce. Two tablespoonfuls of rum and one of finely chopped crystallised fruit may be stirred in at the same time as the whipped cream if liked.

CHERRY FLAN

Bake an empty flan case of pâte sucrée (page 84) or sweet short crust pastry, and either stew some cherries or open a tin of them. When cooked or opened drain off the syrup and reduce it by quick boiling until it is really thick, adding a little more sugar if you think it necessary. Add

Bavarian charlotte

a teaspoonful or two of red currant jelly and, if you like it, a few drops of Kirsch or Maraschino. Let this syrup cool, and when it is just the right consistence to spread, pour it over the cherries to make a lovely glistening glaze.

CHERRIES IN RED WINE

Claret-type red wine from various countries is so cheap today that for a special occasion when one wishes to make a hit it is more than possible to buy a half-bottle without feeling guilty of great extravagance.

Remove the stalks and stones from a pound or so of red cherries and put them into a saucepan with enough light red wine to cover them, adding sugar to taste and a tiny pinch of cinnamon.

Bring slowly to the boil and immediately it shows signs of actual boiling, draw the pan off the heat and let the cherries just poach for ten minutes with the lid tightly on.

Let them get cold and then stir in a tablespoonful of melted red currant jelly.

If the syrup does not look thick enough when you take the cherries off the heat, remove them into a dish with a perforated spoon, reduce the syrup to the right thickness by rapid boiling, and let it get cool before adding the melted jelly.

CHERRY TURNOVERS

A speciality from Buckinghamshire which is famous for its black cherries.

225

Short-crust pastry made with lard and $\frac{1}{2}$ lb. flour: $\frac{1}{2}-\frac{3}{4}$ lb. ripe black cherries: granulated sugar.

Wash and stone the cherries and sprinkle them with granulated sugar.

Roll out the pastry an eighth of an inch thick

Duke of Cambridge Tart

and cut into 3–4 inch rounds. Heap up the cherries on the rounds, wet the pastry edge and fold over in half to make a turnover, pinching the edges well together to prevent the juice from escaping.

Bake for about half an hour in a hot oven at first and then at a lower temperature until the pastry is browned. Serve hot or cold, sprinkled with caster sugar.

CHOCOLATE PANCAKES

2 oz. flour : 2 tablespoonfuls milk : 2 egg-whites : 4 egg-yolks : 1 tablespoonful sugar : 2 table-spoonfuls cream : chocolate.

Make a batter with the flour, milk and the eggs beaten separately, yolks and whites. Add the sugar and a pinch of salt and then beat well with two tablespoonfuls of cream. With this batter fry some very thin small pancakes, brown-ing one side only, then lay them on a dish, un-fried side upwards, and grate enough chocolate over them to cover the tops completely.

Now roll them up, dust them with caster sugar and arrange them in a long buttered fireproof dish. Bake in a moderate oven for twenty minutes and serve at once.

DUKE OF CAMBRIDGE TART

A particularly delicious pudding which owes its unusual texture to the fact that the egg mixture must be boiled.

6 oz. short crust pastry : 3 oz. unsalted butter : 3 oz. caster sugar : 2 yolks of eggs : crystallised fruit.

Mix the butter, sugar and eggs together in a small saucepan and line a sponge tin with the pastry. Spread on the bottom of this a layer of chopped crystallised fruit or candied peel, bring the mixture in the saucepan to the boil and pour it boiling over the fruit. Then bake in a moderate oven until the top is a rich crinkly brown and eat hot, though for a picnic cold is not impossible.

GREEN GOOSEBERRY PUDDING

Gooseberry pies and fools are not the only sweets made with these welcome early fruits.

A quart measure of green gooseberries : $\frac{1}{2}$ oz. butter : 1 egg : $\frac{1}{4}$ pint breadcrumbs : sugar to taste : 8 oz. short-crust pastry.

Top and tail the gooseberries, wash them and stew them in as little water as possible until tender. Then rub them through a sieve and mix with them the butter, beaten egg, breadcrumbs and sugar. Line a pie-dish with the pastry (Volume One, page 84), fill it with the gooseberry mixture and bake in a moderate oven for about forty minutes.

Serve with custard or cream.

GUARDS PUDDING

One of the greatest favourites of my childhood. It *had* to be made with raspberry jam, though some wrongly prefer strawberry.

3 oz. breadcrumbs : 2 oz. caster sugar : 2 oz. melted butter : 3 oz. raspberry jam : 3 eggs : 1 saltspoonful of bicarbonate of soda.

Mix all the dry ingredients in a bowl and then add the jam and butter. Beat in the eggs one by one and lastly add the sieved bicarbonate of soda.

Turn into a buttered pudding-basin and steam for two hours.

Extra warmed jam can be served with it, but I think it is nicer with a little caster sugar sprinkled over the pudding and a dish of clotted cream at hand.

HEDGEHOG TRIFLE

An extremely fanciful dish, delicious to eat, which will earn the approbation of right-minded children of all ages.

1 stale oval-shaped sponge cake : wine or fruit juice for soaking : raisins : 3 oz. blanched sweet almonds : $\frac{1}{2}$ pint custard : 2 tablespoonfuls red currant jelly or other suitable jam.

Cut the sponge cake into a hedgehog shape and put it into the serving dish. Scoop a piece out of the middle of the back (keeping it carefully) and fill this cavity now and then with the fruit syrup or the wine or both, and when the cake has absorbed enough put the bit back in place. Stick in two raisins or sultanas in the proper place to mark the eyes and split the almonds into two or three thin strips each and brown them lightly in the oven. Cover the entire back of the hedgehog with these splinters,

227

sloping them slightly backwards, and when it is all completed pour a custard round him, putting a couple of spoonfuls of the jam in front of his nose to make it look as if he is eating it. Whipped cream, suitably flavoured, could be used instead of the custard if this is to be a party piece.

KENTISH APPLE PIE

1½ lb. cooking apples : 4 oz. caster sugar : 4 oz. cheddar cheese : 4 cloves : 6 oz. short crust pastry.

Cut the peeled and cored apples into thick slices and put a layer of these into a pie-dish. Sprinkle with a tablespoonful of the sugar and then add the rest of the apple and sugar and add the cloves here and there. Pour in half a tea-cupful of water.

Cover the apples with the cheese cut in thin slices, and sprinkle with a tiny dust of pepper, a little grated nutmeg and half a teaspoonful of caster sugar.

Cover with the pastry and bake in a moderately hot oven for forty minutes or so. Serve hot.

BAKED ORANGES

5 seedless oranges : 1½ lb. granulated sugar : 4 oz. butter : 2 cloves.

Wash the oranges and boil them unpeeled in a quart or so of water on a very low heat until the skins are soft, the water covering them all the time. It will take about three hours.

As soon as they are cool enough to handle, cut them in halves across with a stainless steel knife, and arrange the halves in a fireproof dish, side by side with the cut side upmost. Meanwhile make a syrup by boiling the sugar with three-quarters of a pint of water for four minutes after the sugar has dissolved, and pour this over the oranges. Dot each half with a flake of the butter, add the cloves to the syrup, and bake in a slow oven for about an hour, basting very frequently. By the time the oranges are done, the syrup should have practically all been absorbed. Serve cold.

ORANGES AND MACAROONS

Peel and slice into pithless sections as many oranges as you want, put them into a glass dish and add as much caster sugar as will sweeten them to your taste.

Leave them for a little to absorb the sugar and then scatter over the top plenty of crushed macaroon or ratafia biscuits, cover this layer with whipped cream and sprinkle more macaroon crumbs over the top of that.

BUTTERED PEARS

Peel and core some dessert pears and cut them in very thin slivers. Put these in a fireproof dish in layers, putting between each layer a sprinkling of sugar and a few thin flakes of unsalted butter. Bake in a slow oven until the top is browned, and serve hot with cream.

Apples can be buttered in the same way, the addition of a very little powdered cinnamon to the sugar being an improvement.

PEPPERMINT PEARS

This unusual American recipe is surprisingly pleasant.

6 dessert pears: 6 oz. sugar: 2 tablespoonfuls crème de menthe: green colouring.

Boil the sugar in half a pint of water for five minutes, then add the crème de menthe and green colouring.

In this poach the peeled, halved and cored pears for about a quarter of an hour until they are tender and coloured green. Serve hot or cold. These pears are often served in America as an accompaniment to hot or cold roast lamb, a sweeter substitute for our own mint sauce.

PINEAPPLE SWEET

Pineapple rings: Madeira cake: sugar syrup: rum: icing sugar: apricot jam.

Stew some round slices of fresh pineapple, or warm some tinned pineapple rings in a sugar syrup flavoured with a little rum, and cut some slices from a stale Madeira cake as nearly as possible the same size as the rings. Fry these lightly in butter, dust them over with icing sugar and coat one side with warmed apricot jam, and arrange on a serving dish.

Drain the pineapple well and place a slice on each piece of Madeira. Thicken the syrup by

Pineapple sweet

boiling it down to the right thickness and pour this over this attractive sweet. Serve it hot.

SUPERIOR ORANGE JELLY

The rinds and juice of six oranges and two lemons: 1 lb. caster sugar: 1 oz. powdered gelatine: 1½ pints water.

Boil the sugar with the water for a few minutes and then add the gelatine after first dissolving it in a little hot water.

Peel the rinds from the oranges and lemon *very* thinly and strain their juice over them.

Now pour the boiling syrup over and allow to stand for an hour. Then strain into a mould and allow to set. It has the most simple and fragrant taste imaginable.

229

Ice-cream

The tiring days of the old-fashioned bucket ice-cream freezer have long been over, and now we have the neat and unobtrusive refrigerator to help us with one of the most delicious of sweet courses.

Most possessors of this happy adjunct to the kitchen will have instructive leaflets from the manufacturer, and each summer will be comforted or perplexed, according to temperament, by the plethora of advice from the women's magazines.

It would not be right, however, if reference to this cold cooking, as the electrical manufacturers have christened it, were to be omitted.

In general, the freezing of ices should start from scratch, that is at the coldest freezing-point in the refrigerator. Some mixtures will freeze more quickly than others, but to begin with, let the mixture be frozen fairly firmly at this lowest temperature, which will take an hour to an hour and a half, according to the richness of the ingredients. When firm take it out, empty into a chilled bowl, add cream, white of egg, etc. as directed in the particular recipe and beat together until frothy.

If the mixture is a rich one, leave the control at hard freezing and put back the trayfuls until the contents reach the right consistence for serving. Then turn the control back to normal and the mixture will remain at the right temperature until wanted.

If the mixture is a thinner one, turn the control back to about half-freeze until it is the right consistence; then as before turn back to normal and keep until wanted.

It is most important to the ease in making ices that everything that is used in the making should be chilled to start with, e.g. whipped cream, whisked egg-whites, custard and sieved fruit. Gelatine when used should be just dissolved and not boiled.

It is also important to keep strictly to the recipe you are using, especially in regard to the quantity of sugar, for its too great preponderance is a hindrance in freezing.

Also note that so far as water ices are concerned they do not need to be turned out and beaten. They demand no more than a few stirrings in the tray itself.

VANILLA ICE-CREAM (1)

$\frac{1}{2}$ pint cream : 2 egg-yolks : 2 oz. caster sugar : $\frac{1}{4}$ pint milk : vanilla essence to taste.

Whisk egg-yolks and sugar well together : mix in very gradually all the milk, whisk all together again, and put the mixture back into the double saucepan and simmer gently for a quarter of an hour, when it will thicken slightly. Stir if there is any danger of it boiling. Now let the mixture get cold, flavour with vanilla and stir in the cream which must be only half-whipped. Pour into the refrigerator trays and freeze without stirring. For a less expensive version—evaporated milk may be used instead of cream.

VANILLA ICE-CREAM (2)

For the custard : $\frac{1}{2}$ pint milk : 1 egg : $\frac{1}{2}$ pint cream : 3 oz. caster sugar : vanilla essence to taste.

Beat the yolk of the egg lightly, adding vanilla, then pour on the boiled milk, cooking in the double saucepan until the custard slightly thickens.

Leave to cool and when it is quite cold beat in the whipped cream and lastly fold in the stiffly whisked egg-white. Freeze at the coldest freezing-point, stirring after the first twenty minutes. Here again—evaporated milk may be substituted for the cream.

LEMON WATER ICE

Water ices are coming back into fashion once more, and what can be more refreshing on a hot summer's day? In this recipe the use of gelatine acts as a binder and produces a more satisfactory texture.

$\frac{1}{4}$ lb. lump sugar : $\frac{1}{2}$ pint water : $\frac{1}{4}$ pint lemon juice : 1 egg-white : $\frac{1}{4}$ oz. powdered gelatine.

Rub the rind of the lemons with the sugar, and then dissolve the sugar in the water and boil quickly for five minutes. Let this syrup get cold and then chill it in the refrigerator. Now add to it the lemon juice and the gelatine dissolved in a very little water, and freeze to a mush at the coldest temperature, which will take at least an hour. Add the beaten egg-white, freeze again for an hour and beat quickly. Freeze for another two hours.

OMELETTE SURPRISE

One of the most exciting ice-cream dishes, and one which is by no means too difficult for the ordinary hostess to make, is the Omelette Surprise, which in fact is ice-cream covered by a hot meringue mixture, a real boon to the enterprising woman who wants to make a name as a first-class cook among her friends.

It should be made with an oval piece of sponge cake, which represents the omelette shape, but for convenience this could be rectangular to be better suited for the use of a block of commercial ice-cream.

In any case the cake should be an inch and a half thick and it should be placed on a solid baking-tin first lined with several thicknesses of heavy kitchen paper, the object of this being to insulate the ice-cream from heat coming from below. The ice-cream should be placed on top of the cake, allowing half an inch of the cake to protrude at the sides and ends, with as much rapidity as possible and quickly covered with ordinary meringue mixture (Volume One, page 116), smoothing it to a level thickness of two-thirds of an inch and completely masking the ice-cream as well as the cake at the sides and ends. It is then placed in a very hot oven, so that the meringue can colour slightly without the ice melting. Five minutes at the very most should achieve this. Any kind of ice-cream can be used and there are a number of varieties of which these are two :

Omelette Surprise Elizabeth

The ice-cream is mixed with crystallised violets and the meringue decorated with the same before it is put into the oven.

Omelette Surprise Milord

The ice-cream (vanilla) is alternated with layers of well drained and iced stewed or tinned pears.

Other mixtures can be well devised.

If small individual portions of the same fascinating preparation are preferred, thick slices or rounds of sponge cake can be hollowed out to make a shell or box, this can be filled with ice-cream, coated with meringue and baked in the same way.

A FEW SUGGESTIONS

A great many people prefer to buy their ice-cream ready-made, and keep it in the refrigerator until wanted. This may get a little monotonous after a while, and a few suggestions for serving it in ways a little more exciting than just dishing it up are appended.

Sundaes have been popular for very many years now and offer the simplest ways of doing this:

Banana sundae: place the two long halves of the banana on the dish with the ice-cream in the middle. Put a little thick cherry syrup or diluted cherry jam on the top of the ice-cream and sprinkle with chopped almonds.

Berry sundae: this consists of alternate spoonfuls of fresh, tinned or frozen berries, such as strawberries or raspberries, in a glass and topping them with whipped cream.

Cherry sundae: put some poached and sweetened stoned red cherries, or tinned ones or maraschino cherries round some vanilla ice-cream in a glass and pour a little thick syrup over.

Chocolate sundae: cover the vanilla ice-cream with cold creamy chocolate sauce, and finish with whipped cream and chopped nuts.

Peach sundae: serve vanilla ice-cream in glasses lined with sliced peaches and finish with a topping of whipped cream.

For a very special occasion something rather grander may be needed, and here we have the assistance of the nineteenth century when the naming of ices was in its heyday. Witness the following, then:

Coupe Alexandra: fruit salad flavoured with Kirsch and surmounted by a strawberry ice-cream.

Coupe Andalouse: sections of orange soaked in maraschino and covered with a lemon ice.

Coupe Brésilienne: pineapple dice soaked in maraschino and covered with a lemon ice.

Coupe Edna May: vanilla ice-cream on a bed of compote of cherries, covered with whipped cream flavoured with raspberries.

Coupe Jacques: fruit salad flavoured with Kirsch covered one half with strawberry ice-cream, the other half with lemon ice with a peeled grape between the two.

233

Coupe Jamaïque: Coffee ice-cream on a bed of pineapple dice soaked in rum, the top sprinkled with a little coarsely ground roasted coffee beans.

Coupe Montmorency: vanilla ice-cream on a bed of brandied cherries.

Coupe Niçoise: fruit salad flavoured with orange Curaçao and covered with orange ice.

Coupe Royale: fruit salad flavoured with Kirsch covered with vanilla ice-cream.

An easier way of giving your home-made ice-cream a special hall-mark of your own is to add to the mixture a little liqueur of some kind to heighten the flavour. In these days of miniature bottles, nothing could be easier, and we do not have to go to the expense of buying more of the liqueur than we need. For cream ices this is added to taste, but for water ices the usual proportion is rather less than $\frac{1}{8}$ pint of the liqueur to a pint of the liquid, a quantity that can easily be reduced to fit our momentary needs.

The liqueur must, of course be one which has an affinity with the main ingredient, for example :

with Cherry, Kirsch or Cherry Brandy

with Oranges, Curaçao, Grand Marnier or Cointreau

with Peaches, Maraschino

with Pineapple, Kirsch or Rum

with Raspberries, Kirsch

with Strawberries, Maraschino.

Coffee ice-cream is wonderful with the addition of a spot of Tia Maria and the same liqueur will give a remarkable touch of flavour to a chocolate ice-cream

BROWN BREAD ICE-CREAM

This is really old-fashioned English.

Cut some stale brown bread in thin slices and dry them in the oven. Pound and sift them through a sieve, and add them to a vanilla ice-cream mixture in the proportion of a teacupful of the crumbs to a quart of the mixture. Mix well together and freeze.

Cakes

BRANDY SNAPS

2 tablespoonfuls golden syrup : 1¾ oz. flour : 1¾ oz. caster sugar : ½ teaspoonful ground ginger : 2 oz. butter : ½ teaspoonful grated lemon rind : ½ teaspoonful brandy.

Melt the syrup, sugar and butter in a saucepan, and stir in the flour sieved with the ginger, the lemon rind and the brandy. Mix well together and drop in small teaspoonfuls on a greased baking sheet about three inches apart, as they will spread.

Bake in a cool oven from seven to ten minutes, and when slightly set, roll each at once round the greased handle of a wooden spoon. You must catch them as soon as they are possible to handle, as if they are cooked too much, they will be too brittle to roll.

Some people like to serve these when cold with a filling of whipped cream, but far too rich for me !

CHOCOLATE TRUFFLES

It would be impertinent of me to attempt a recipe for these delicious chocolate fancies which could in any way compare with the professional version, but here is one which can be made at home with some success.

4½ oz. praline (page 236) : 4½ oz. plain cooking chocolate : 2 oz. butter : chocolate icing : cocoa and icing sugar mixed in equal quantities.

Warm the chocolate to a paste, add the butter

Brandy snaps

235

and mix well with the praline. Leave until the mixture is firm but not hard and roll into balls the size of large marbles with fingers dusted with icing sugar. When these are firm and set roll them in the mixture of cocoa and icing sugar.

A few drops of rum may be added to the truffle mixture, if liked.

Praline: $2\frac{1}{2}$ oz. caster sugar : $2\frac{1}{2}$ oz. unblanched sweet almonds or hazel nuts.

Rub the nuts well in a damp cloth and put them with the sugar in a small heavy saucepan, stirring them lightly over heat until the sugar has become a coffee-coloured caramel and the nuts are well grilled. Turn out on to an oiled marble slab and leave to cool. When cold pound this pralin to a powder and use as above.

Chocolate Icing: make as Butter Icing, page 115, with grated chocolate added.

COCONUT CONES

3 egg-whites : 6 oz. desiccated coconut : 10 oz. caster sugar : rice paper.

Whisk the whites of eggs stiffly, then add the sugar and coconut. Put the rice paper on a baking sheet and pile up the mixture in the shape of cones. Bake in a cool oven until they get a very pale fawn colour and leave to cool. Half the mixture may be coloured pink before baking, if liked.

COTTAGE CHEESE PIE

236 Tartlets and pies are not always filled with fresh cream, as witness our own old-fashioned cheesecakes. Of recent years we have learned a good deal from America about the making of this sort of dish which is so useful either as a sweet or as a cake. Here is an example.

$\frac{1}{2}$ pint cottage cheese : 1 egg : $\frac{1}{8}$ pint cream : 1 teaspoonful melted butter : 1 oz. caster sugar : 1 tablespoonful chopped blanched almonds : pastry.

Mash up the cheese, add the egg and beat well together. Add the rest of the ingredients and mix well. Pour this mixture into a flan case lined with what kind of pastry you prefer and bake in a good oven until the filling is quite firm, about half an hour. Sprinkle when done and still hot with icing sugar mixed with a little powdered cinnamon, and leave for about three-quarters of an hour, when it should be eaten warm.

GATEAU SAINT-HONORÉ

This is the queen of all cream-filled patisseries, and requires only patience and care to make it.

For the short crust : use 3 oz. flour : 2 oz. butter : $\frac{1}{2}$ teaspoonful caster sugar : 1 egg-yolk and water ; for the filling : whipped sweetened cream : chopped blanched pistachio nuts for the choux paste, see Volume One, page 94: caramel sugar.

Roll the pastry out to a round of eight inches diameter, and damp a band of half an inch round the edge with slightly-beaten egg-white. Pipe a circle of choux paste round this edge with a $\frac{3}{4}$-inch plain forcer, joining it neatly. Pipe the rest of the choux paste into about a dozen small balls.

Now bake the shell and the little balls apart from it, the shell for about forty minutes in a moderate oven and the balls until they are quite crisp and hard, when they should be removed.

When the cake is cold, fill the centre with the whipped cream and decorate round the edge with the choux paste balls, either glazed with caramel sugar (see below) or brushed over with apricot jam and rolled in chopped pistachio nuts, which have first been blanched in the same way as sweet almonds.

If liked, the little balls may have first been filled with the same cream as that used for the main filling, but there can of course be many variations of the fillings concerned.

Finally, if liked, more chopped pistachios may be scattered on top of the main filling,

Caramel sugar

Put half a pound of granulated sugar into a small heavy saucepan with an eighth of a pint of water and a small pinch of salt, let it dissolve completely and then boil it without stirring until it begins to colour a light brown. It may then be used as a glaze.

GINGER BISCUITS

$\frac{1}{2}$ lb. flour: 2 oz. sugar: 1 teaspoonful baking powder: 2 tablespoonfuls treacle or golden syrup: 3 oz. fat: $\frac{1}{2}$ oz. or so ground ginger: mixed spice.

Sieve together flour, ginger, baking powder and spice to taste. Rub in the fat and add the sugar. Now add the warmed treacle and make all into a dough.

Roll out a quarter of an inch thick, and cut in rounds.

Bake on a greased baking tin in a moderate oven for ten to twenty minutes.

GLOUCESTERSHIRE EASTER CAKES

These extremely attractive large biscuits were often made in old days at Easter time, when two or three were tied together with bright different coloured ribbons.

$4\frac{1}{2}$ oz. butter: 3 oz. caster sugar: 2 egg-yolks: 1 scant oz. currants: 1 tablespoonful brandy or rum: 6 oz. plain flour: 1 large pinch salt: an eighth teaspoonful each powdered cinnamon and mixed spice.

Cream the butter, add the sugar and cream again. Then beat in the egg-yolks, one by one, mix in the currants and add the rum or brandy.

Mix in the flour sieved with the salt and spices, and knead to a pliable paste. Flour a board and roll it out about an eighth of an inch thick, cutting into fluted rounds about five inches in diameter.

Bake on a lightly greased baking-tin for about twenty minutes in a moderate oven. They should be a pale fawn colour when done. Just before

237

they are done, brush each with slightly whisked egg-white, dust quickly with caster sugar and finish the cooking.

They are extraordinarily nice.

MACAROONS

¼ lb. ground almonds : 1 oz. rice flour : ½ lb. caster sugar : 3 small egg-whites : vanilla essence : blanched almonds split into halves.

Beat the egg-whites very lightly and add the rest of the ingredients to them, except the blanched almond halves, mixing to a stiff paste.

Put small walnut-sized balls of this on a sheet of rice paper on a baking-tin, leaving room for spreading. Brush each with cold water and place a blanched almond half on each.

Bake in a moderate oven for twenty to thirty minutes.

For **Chocolate Macaroons** add to the mixture an ounce and a half of grated chocolate which has been warmed in the oven.

MAIDS OF HONOUR

These delightful little cakes have always been a great speciality of Richmond in Surrey. The curd need not nowadays be made at home, for it can readily be bought under the name of Cottage Cheese.

¼ lb. cottage cheese : 3 oz. butter : 2 yolks of eggs : 3 oz. caster sugar : 1½ oz. ground almonds : the grated rind and juice of a lemon : ½ teaspoon-ful almond essence : ½ nutmeg, grated : 1 heaped tablespoonful cold mashed potato : 8 oz. puff pastry (Volume One, page 88).

Sieve the cottage cheese with the butter. Beat up the yolks, add the sugar and beat well. Add now the mashed potato, ground almonds, grated rind and juice of the lemon, the essence and nutmeg. Mix these all well together and then add them gradually to the cottage cheese and butter mixture.

Line about three dozen patty tins with puff paste, and fill each three-quarters full with the mixture. Bake for twenty-five to thirty minutes until the filling is set and a beautiful golden-brown.

MARBLE CAKE

8 oz. flour : ¼ lb. fat : 6–8 oz. sugar : 3 eggs : ½ teaspoonful baking powder : ⅛ pint milk.

Make as directed under Rich Cake on page 124, and when mixed divide into three or four portions, colouring one pink, another green, another with chocolate and one left plain.

Grease a six-inch cake tin and fill it with alternate spoonfuls to give the right marbled effect when cooked.

Bake in a moderate oven for an hour and a half.

MERINGUE PIE

1 teaspoonful white vinegar : 1 teaspoonful vanilla essence : 1 teaspoonful cold water : 3

well-whisked egg-whites: $4\frac{1}{2}$ oz. icing sugar sieved with an eighth teaspoonful salt and half a teaspoonful baking powder : fresh fruit : cream.

Mix the water, vinegar and vanilla in a small cup. Add the sugar to the egg-whites, half a teaspoonful at a time, and as you beat in the sugar add alternately a few drops of the mixture in the cup. When all is added, go on beating the mixture for several minutes.

Now butter and flour a sponge tin, heap the meringue mixture on it and with a spatula or palette knife shape it like an open tart. Bake in a very slow oven until crisp, and when cold and ready to serve, fill the centre with fresh straw-

Meringue pie

CAKES

berries or raspberries or indeed any other suitable fruit in season, cut up if necessary. Coat finally with a good layer of whipped cream, which can be further decorated with fruit if you wish.

A version of this pie in Australia is called a Pavlova Cake.

Pear upside-down cake

PARKIN

7 oz. flour : 3 oz. fat : 2 oz. brown sugar : 2 tablespoonfuls treacle or golden syrup : 4 oz. medium oatmeal : 1 tablespoonful baking powder : $\frac{1}{2}$ teaspoonful mixed spice.

Mix together the flour and oatmeal and rub in the fat. Add the sugar, baking powder and spice

and mix well together. Add a tablespoonful of boiling water to the treacle and mix this into the dry ingredients. Shape into balls the size of a large walnut, put them in a greased baking tin and press a blanched almond-half or a piece of candied lemon peel on each.

Bake in a moderate oven for a quarter of an hour.

PEAR UPSIDE-DOWN CAKE

An easy to make party piece.

6 pear halves : 6 oz. self-raising flour : 2 oz. ground almonds : 5 oz. butter : 4 oz. caster sugar : 2 eggs : milk : vanilla essence : demerara sugar and lemon juice.

Arrange the tinned or fresh dessert pear halves in the bottom of a 7-in. cake tin, sprinkle them with demerara sugar and lemon juice.

Cream 4 oz. of the sugar and the butter together and beat in half the lightly beaten eggs. Then fold in the flour and the almonds which you will have sifted together, alternating with the rest of the egg and a little milk until you have a smooth consistency. Melt the remaining ounce of butter and pour it over the pears, then drop in the cake mixture. Bake in a medium oven for 15 minutes, turning it down to slow for another 50 minutes. Turn out onto a wire tray with the pears at the top, and when cool decorate with cherries and whipped cream if desired.

OAT FINGERS (OR FLAPJACKS)

4 oz. coarse porridge oats : 2 oz. butter : 3 oz. sugar : 1 teaspoonful treacle or golden syrup.

Melt the butter and treacle in a saucepan, add the sugar and oats and stir together over a gentle heat for a few moments.

Turn into a buttered baking tin and bake until a nice brown in a moderate oven, which should take from fifteen to twenty minutes.

Let the mixture cool in the tin, then turn it out and cut it into suitable fingers.

SHORTBREAD

6 oz. flour : 5 oz. butter : 2 oz. ground rice : $1\frac{1}{2}$–3 oz. caster sugar.

Sieve the flour with the rice and sugar, rub in the butter, which must be softened, and knead to a pliable dough, adding no liquid whatsoever. Shape into two cakes an inch thick, prick their tops with a fork and put a strip of candied peel on each.

Leave them to mellow for about an hour, then bake in a moderate oven for about forty minutes.

STRAWBERRY SHORTCAKE

An American delicacy which is in process of being adopted.

$\frac{1}{2}$ lb. flour : 2 large teaspoonfuls baking powder : 2 large teaspoonfuls caster sugar : 1 large pinch salt : 2 oz. butter : about $\frac{1}{4}$ pint milk :

241

butter for spreading : $\frac{1}{4}$ pint cream : $\frac{3}{4}$ lb. strawberries : caster sugar.

Mash up the strawberries, sweeten with caster sugar to taste and leave the mixture to stand for an hour.

Sieve together the flour, sugar, salt and baking powder and rub in the butter. Mix to a soft but not sticky dough with the milk. Pat or knead the dough lightly on a floured board, roll it out a quarter of an inch thick, prick it well with a fork and cut it into $2\frac{1}{2}$ inch rounds. Spread one with a little softened butter and place the other on top. Bake in a hot oven until delicately browned and done, then split open across and leave to get cold on a wire tray. Butter again, cover with the mashed fruit, put the second half on top and heap more fruit on top of this. Or you can divide the dough in half, roll each out to a round, bake these in two sandwich tins and serve as a large cake in the same way as the small ones above.

A richer cake can be made by increasing the butter to three ounces and adding one or two beaten egg-yolks to the milk for mixing.

The same can, of course, be done with raspberries.

TARTLETS COEUR À LA CRÈME

As a result of the First World War and the stream of Belgian refugees that arrived in this country it was not many years before Belgian patisserie rose to become a prime favourite among us. Until then we had been satisfied with our own cooked cheesecakes made with curds, but now we were to sample the delights of various pastries filled with uncooked cream. The following is quite a good example of this sort of thing.

For the cases: sweet short crust described in Volume One, page 84, or as follows:
4 oz. plain flour: 2 oz. caster sugar: 2 oz. butter: 2 egg-yolks: pinch of salt, which will make a dozen tartlets.

Line the tartlet tins with the pastry, prick the bottoms and bake blind for five to seven minutes, at 375° F or Gas No. 5.

Pass 2 oz. of soured cream or cream cheese through a wire sieve and add caster sugar to taste, and when the tartlets are cold fill them with this mixture and cover it with small ripe strawberries. Brush these over carefully with warmed red currant jelly, and serve as soon as this sets.

The French have several delicious ways of using cream or cream cheese with the addition of egg-whites, and though these are usually served as they are, they could well be used as a basic filling for these little tartlets if desired. Here are two of them. They both will need a container with holes in the bottom for the cream to drain and special French ones can sometimes be bought. But a small deep pie tin can be substituted if a few holes are punched in the bottom.

Crémets

Whip stiffly half a pint of double cream and fold in two egg-whites beaten as for a soufflé. Line

Tartlets coeur à la crème

your pierced mould with a square of clean butter muslin, turn the cream into this and fold over the corners on top. Stand the mould so that the contents can drain and leave it in a cool larder until the next day. Serve turned out and covered with fresh unwhipped cream and hand plenty of sugar. Lovely with strawberries.

Fromage à la crème

Put half a pound of unsalted cream cheese or alternatively cottage cheese into a bowl and mash it smoothly with a fork or pass it through a sieve. Add a tablespoonful of caster sugar and mash again. Now mix in three stiffly beaten egg-whites as in making a soufflé, and turn into your pierced muslin-lined mould, as above. Leave in the refrigerator for a couple of hours, then turn it out on to a plate, pour about a quarter of a pint of thick cream over it and hand caster sugar separately.

Index

245

INDEX

INDEX

INDEX

INDEX